SOUTHERN NIGHTS AND THE LIGHT OF AWARENESS

BY PETER CALVERT & KEITH HILL

PETER CALVERT
Guided Healing
Agapé and the Hierarchy of Love

PETER CALVERT & KEITH HILL
The Kosmic Web
On Acquiring Wisdom
The Matapaua Conversations
Learning Who You Are

PETER CALVERT, RICHARD BENTLEY
CAROLYN LONGDEN, TRISHA WREN
People of the Earth

KEITH HILL
The New Mysticism
Experimental Spirituality
How Did I End Up Here?

Southern Nights and the Light of Awareness

Peter Calvert

Edited by Keith Hill

attar books

First published by Attar Books 2025
Copyright © Peter Calvert + Keith Hill 2025

The moral rights of the authors have been asserted.

Paperback ISBN 978-1-0670142-6-1
Hardcover ISBN 978-1-0670142-7-8

Cover image: James Stone, Shutterstock

All rights reserved. Copying and distributing passages excerpted from this book for the purpose of sharing and debating is permitted on the condition that (1) the source of each excerpt is fully acknowledged and (2) the excerpts are given not sold, ie. the process is non-commercial. Otherwise, except for fair dealing or brief passages quoted in a newspaper, magazine, radio, television or internet review, no part of this book may be reproduced in any form or by any means without permission in writing from the Publisher.

Attar Books
Auckland, New Zealand
www.attarbooks.com

Contents

Introduction: An Accidental Mystic   7

1   **Restating Fundamental Principles**   17
Accessing spiritual education ■ Cancelling the idea of divinity ■ Experience, confusion, knowledge

2   **Developing Spiritual Awareness**   26
Conditions for acquiring direct knowledge ■ The physical and the spiritual ■ Untaught knowing ■ Union with one of this transmission's two sources ■ Questions about divinity

3   **Spirituality, Science, Religion**   37
Sciences and spiritual experience ■ The argument against religion

4   **Origin of the Swastika**   43
The cross and the swastika ■ A long-standing error ■ Detaching historical usage from 21st century usage

5   **A Universal Model of Existence**   49
Instructions for the model's development ■ Rethinking Indra's Net ■ Corollary 1: Establishing a fresh perspective ■ Corollary 2: Unlinking historical interpretations ■ Corollary 3: Nullifying a historical injunction ■ Corollary 4: The wider impact of this annulment ■ Corollary 5: Adopting a planetary perspective ■ Corollary 6: Adopting a multi-life perspective ■ Corollary 7: Indra's Net updated ■ Corollary 8: Dependent origination and dying

6	**A New Vision**	64
	On countering state-dependent memory ■ An address to Peter ■ More on the multiverse model ■ Model: Species' willingness to bequest agapé	

7	**Dependent origination**	71
	Yet more on the multiverse model ■ Dependent origination relationship ■ Further clarification	

8	**Internal and emotional self-cleansing**	77
	A disturbing dream ■ "Darkness is greater than light" ■ Power, choice, decision ■ Work-life balance, 1000 year support ■ Golf guidance	

9	**Life in Spirit**	86
	Being contented ■ Becoming ■ Gathering informational riches	

10	**Metaphors of Agapéic Space**	96
	Mussel farm model ■ Recognising a soulmate ■ Spiritual formation	

11	**Protocols for Meditation**	103
	Meditation group protocols ■ Lingering spirits and elementals	

12	**The Triple Screen Model**	107
	The triple screen model ■ Perceiving a reintegrated node ■ Choosing appropriate language	

13	**Violence, Love, Wisdom**	119
	Political violence ■ Accumulating love and wisdom	

	Epilogue	124
	Appendix: Nodes of Dao-Consciousness	127
	Glossary	133
	Further reading	139

INTRODUCTION

—┼─┼—

An Accidental Mystic

The first time I saw an aura was during the Third Theosophical Centennial Convention, held at Whanganui Lodge from 3rd to 7th January, 1997. I had had glimpses of auras over the previous five years, once in a dream, and several times in the altered states of consciousness involved in laying-on-of-hands energy work, but this was my first unequivocal, open-eyed, daylight perception of a human aura.

It occurred on the third day of the convention. During the first two days I had gone out of my way to meet as many people as I could, so by the third day I was feeling particularly relaxed. That afternoon, while settling into a chair in the first row, I noticed Gavin behind me. I greeted him, saying something like, "I'm feeling good today. Not afraid to sit in the front row!" For some undefined reason it seemed the right place to be. As the speaker began, my thought drifted to a discussion of auras that occurred earlier in the day, and I wondered if I would be able to see the speaker's aura.

The Lodge had been converted from a small factory. Skylight panels in the roof were the dominant light source. It was afternoon, on a partly clouded day, and the skylights provided the room with a bright and largely shadow-free illumination. I was sitting on the extreme left of the front row. Due to the shape of the room, from where I was I could see the freshly-painted opposite wall extending three to four metres behind the speaker. This proved to be an excellent background for discerning an aura.

I had some idea of how to look and what to look for, having read other people's accounts of seeing an aura. I knew it was helpful to have a relaxed body as well as a relaxed state of mind, and not to be concerned whether or not I was successful. It was necessary to neither peer nor squint, and not to focus on the body but on its outline. I expected the aura not to be seen directly, but through the way it modified the density of the background. I had also read that the aura changed fluidly to reflect emotions and thoughts. However, I had never been able to imagine what that fluidity might look like, having only ever seen static representations on the printed page. So whatever I saw, I expected it to be subtle. And subtle it certainly was.

After looking unsuccessfully for a while, I began to move my eyes around. I noticed, as expected, the optical after-image move with my eye position. Then I started to notice a quiet shining region close to the outline of the speaker's body, that stayed stable in both central and peripheral vision, and seemed, very subtly, to glow. It didn't emit light, more seeming to add a curious clarity to the visual features of the wall behind his body. It was almost as if other wavelengths of light were present, ultraviolet light perhaps, that were just beyond the threshold of my perception but that somehow modified what I was seeing.

During the twenty-seven years I have worked with scientific instruments I operated two that depend on stable flames for their operation. Chemists will be familiar with them, as they are basic tools of modern analytic chemistry: the atomic absorption spectrometer, also used for flame emission analysis, and the inductively coupled plasma spectrometer. Much atomic information is carried in the ultraviolet wavelength range, with the flames they measure being pale blue to almost invisible, yet teeming with energy. The speaker's inner auric layer reminded me of those flames. In modern descriptions the aura has been likened to a plasma, a high-temperature flame-like state of gas, and it seemed so to me, but only on the innermost layers. My perception additionally involved a dimension that was somehow structured more finely than normal four-dimensional physical reality.

I had for years wondered if observations of the aura were like an optical after-image, the image of the complementary colour that endures after a bright object or light is seen, i.e. after a camera flash. After-images maintain a constant position in the visual field, and so move with the eye, rather than stay anchored in the viewed scene. As my perception of the aura grew clearer, I was able to differentiate between the after-image, which faded and moved with my eyes, and the fine shimmering field around the speaker, which didn't fade and remained around him.

As the speaker continued, I noticed gentle variations in the extent to which his inner aura stayed close to the outline of his physical body, or extended beyond it, especially around his head and upper back. The variations seemed to correspond with the emotional content, tone of his speech, and manner of delivery. At one point it extended about half a metre out from behind his shoulders.

On many occasions previously I had felt accumulations of hot, sticky or viscous energy at different locations on the bodies of people with whom I was conducting laying-on-of-hands healing. I had also seen illustrations of such accumulations, so it was with a feeling of delight that I noticed a small cloudy area behind his neck. At last I was perceiving visually what had been so apparent to my hands!

It was at about this time I noticed that the wall behind the speaker's back was a beautiful pale clear green, and that the green grew smoothly and progressively deeper into a mid-green hue the further it extended behind him from his body, only disappearing where my view was interrupted by the kitchen wall. At the time I didn't pay much attention to the subtle green hue, assuming either light patterns in the room contributed to the variation in colour density, or that whoever painted the wall had been extremely skilful.

Throughout the convention, I was staying in a little cabin in the camping ground. When I woke the next morning the colour of the wall behind the speaker came back to mind, and something seemed wrong. It somehow seemed too classy a paint job was required to achieve such a seamless transition of colour density over three to four metres of wall. Later, at breakfast with the other participants, I found Bee Brown, then president of the Wanganui Lodge. I knew she had chosen what colour the walls were to be painted, so asked if they were green. She said, "Oh no, just off-white." I then realised that the subtly deepening green hue I had seen was an outer region of the speaker's aura. It had incorporated such a quality of stillness, I had interpreted what I was seeing as a property of the wall!

On one other occasion I saw an internal image which contained that same property of stillness, to the degree it became timeless. I understood that the quality of stillness I experienced as a component of the aura carried the information, this is not just how it looks for now, or even for a long time, but forever. I assume this is the quality referred to by those who write of glimpsing eternity. There seems to be a subtle distinction to be made between this and time being absent, which indicates to me it is a perception of non-physical reality.

I feel insufficient certainty about this to be able to state any conclusion definitively, but I tentatively conclude that the speaker's outer aura contained information about him (or was him) in the non-physical domain, due to its quality of timelessness. Of course, anyone familiar with these perceptions may find my 'fumbling after meaning' amusing, but I trust them to be compassionate with it.

I had been wanting to see subtle realities for many years, and had felt frustrated in my failed attempts to do so. It is clear now that there were factors acting beyond my conscious control that influenced my ability to perceive those realities. So such perceptions always feel like a precious gift, and that if I take the time to notice them and reflect on what I have seen, then I will be given more. That Theosophical convention created a suitable environment for such a gift to be received.

I never meant to be a mystic. It crept up on me, like a moat surreptitiously and progressively dug around a castle, eventually leaving me isolated. All while thinking I was normal, or as normal as one can be in a lower middle-class home in New Zealand with pretensions to being at least upper middle-class. But the work called me to take it up. So I did. My mother would see it as claptrap. She believed that hell was here on Earth, and when you died you went into a hole in the ground and stayed there.

My father never told me until the last year of his long life that he had left all that spiritual stuff behind when he went to Auckland after the war to build his wife and children a home. "There was no room for it," he said. Building the house on evenings and weekends on reverted farmland, using the timber milled from macrocarpa trees growing on the land, while they lived first in a tent, then an old army hut, left him short of talking time. At least about things like karma and spirits that he had learned from his mother.

She had learned about them from the Theosophical Society in Hamilton, where she was an early member. It was a radical organisation then, not the withered remainder it is now. So I dutifully avoided church and pitied Catholics for being so foolish as to believe in something that backwards could be spelled "dog".

Then, over a period of about twenty years, my outlook changed. Some might say I grew up. I certainly avoided that to the extent I could! But partnerships and death caught up with me and reduced me to tears too often. Eventually, I became curious about why my hands got heavy and tired after caressing a lover when it was such easy work. And so I was progressively inducted into understanding the energetics of bodies and life.

Along the way I started to meditate. First at lunchtimes in my room at work, then also in spiritual training groups at night, and later for ten days at a stretch during Vipassana (Buddhist insight) meditation. That really worked well!

Very early in my meditation practice I was approached by unknown identities who asked: "Which path do you choose? The left-hand or the right-hand?" When I didn't decide quickly, they asked again. I chose the right-hand path. Having since met a few people who chose the left-hand path I'm glad I chose the right!

I later received instruction while meditating:

- Training the attention is the essential prerequisite for travel in the domain that may only be discovered when one has forgotten the body and its needs.
- To forget the body, it must be comfortable, relaxed and at peace.
- To be at peace, the body-mind must be calm.
- To be calm, unresolved issues must be minimised.
- The resolution of issues is therefore the first priority.
- When developmental issues, power issues, or interpersonal issues impede the tranquillity, meditation is best avoided in favour of the resolution of such issues.
- When they have been completely or partially resolved, then tranquillity is again possible and meditation may be profitably resumed.

That process has enabled me to reach more deeply inside myself than I had any reason to expect, and to correct tendencies carried through from ancient events that have shaped my present life experience through choices made and avoided. Death by war, murder and torture leave marks upon the soul, and progressively discovering them continues to free me from their thrall.

Discovering and developing my ability to access regions beyond the ordinary mind and identity have shaped the remainder of my life.

Along the way I have been exposed to a series of situations both in and out of body which have taught me not to fear, but instead recognise them as indicators that I am about to learn something important. I haven't always done so successfully, and have often had to drag my heart back out of my throat. Nonetheless, I have sometimes been blessed with the opportunity to learn first-hand of spiritual realities beyond the body. At other times I have listened and written what has been communicated by those in spirit who have sought to know me again.

Such sources have invariably declined to identify themselves by any particular name. I believe there are very good reasons for that. The process of taking dictation from another person can be described by an old word which comes from the Latin language, *amanuensis*. In the context of this book the other person is discarnate and usually unidentifiable and can thereby only communicate in chunks of meaning, usually using words in the language one knows. But not always. Amanuensis is one of a few words previously unknown to me. I first encountered it during this process, so I had to consult a dictionary to find its meaning:

Amanuensis, noun, a literary or artistic assistant, in particular one who takes dictation or copies manuscripts.

Accepting the role of amanuensis has also resulted in me being tested on most occasions I have sat in meditation waiting for dialogue from those who mentor me. Regarding which they stated:

> The person who allows their capacity to be utilised as amanuensis should expect regular testing by the source of the information they receive. This is only reasonable. Every technological communication system is tested routinely for integrity, capacity and error

rate. This is to evaluate its adequacy for the task, and if upgrading is needed. An individual's capacity to function consistently as an amanuensis may lack in various capacities, so they are tested.

For a test to be meaningful it must probe beliefs and associations, and especially fearfulness, for fearlessness is required in this work. Many myths limit an individual's willingness to work with an unknown spiritual other because they amplify the fear that the other's intention is evil.

Tests also address such concerns in order to estimate the extent to which the recipient may edit content from the conveyed information stream at either the conscious or preconscious level.

To set the context for all that follows, I quote from the first material I received while meditating. It outlines the problem that this book and all the other material I have received addresses. The communication is dated 25 March, 1990. Having received an inner call to meditate, I asked why they had come. They responded:

We wish on this occasion to utilise your amanuensis skills. Our work is incomplete. Will you help us?

Peter: Yes.

Good. We begin by adding to our prior communication concerning the historical variations in the way the spiritual domain is understood, and in the ways the impact of the spiritual domain on human existence is studied.

We intend to initiate an international trend towards the study of the spiritual domain on human life in all its variety, with an emphasis on its impact on the theory of being.

Where once human knowledge was focused on agriculture and food production, today theory has expanded to encompass the origins and end of the universe. The question is, what lies beyond them? Anyone who has studied history knows that spiritual impulses have arisen in humanity's breast and mind for many thousands of years. Once it was sufficient to respond only to the heartfelt love emanating from the domain during sleep, via dreams and visions. Now, however, a more dynamic understanding is required, which includes acknowledging the existence of entities who inhabit the spiritual domain and encompasses direct investigation of that domain.

Once a consensus regarding the reality of the spiritual domain is affirmed, derived empirically from the observations of mystics, the world will arrive at a new appreciation of the wholeness of reality. A complete view will then be available to anyone willing to take the time to develop the requisite skills to study it.

This will challenge the old order, it is true. Religion in its simplistic forms will fall away. Belief will be less required. This is not in any sense a bad thing, as empiricism is universally respectful of the individual's right to make up their own mind. Coercion has no place in it.

Respect for the individual is commonplace in civilised societies. Respect may be extended to religious belief as a subset of reality, rather than be considered to lie completely outside it, which is the attitude current among the trendsetters of rational thought, the scientific community. It is to this community that attention must be directed, using rational argument first to promote the empirical reality of the spiritual domain, then to accurately map the consequences for the average person and for those endowed with spiritual perceptions.

The question is, who will help us in our task to promote spiritual empiricism? It cannot be participants in established religious orders, for they would understand it to represent a threat to their continued existence. And it will not be undertaken by conventional scientists and scholars, for they are committed to their existing world view, from which spiritual understanding is excluded, and which they equate with fantasies and dreams.

It will take a new type of person, a mystic who is both scientifically and spiritually trained, who is capable of avoiding the worst excesses of the illusions human beings are naturally prey to, to initiate an informed and rational debate that is grounded in empirical philosophy. Then, and only then, will the scientific community's own principles compel them to attend to the argument. All else is vain crying in the wind.

In 2024 there are now many signs that attending to the evidence is occurring, using the highest quality protocols of observation and analysis. Cooperative research is accelerating across many organisations, e.g., Bigelow Institute, Society for Scientific Exploration, International Association for Near Death Studies, International Network for the Study of Spirituality, Institute for Noetic Sciences, and others in Europe. Their research results are being published in English and many other languages. The net effect is to nudge the emerging paradigm into a profile high enough to provide a robust world view inclusive of consciousness as primary – the 'Ground of all Being'. It is again becoming solid ground on which to stand.

The text for this book was received in Riverton, on the coast of New Zealand's province of Southland. After moving to Gore in Southland with Janet, we became aware the sea was an hour's drive away. Janet, in particular, having had thirty years accessing the sea at Matapaua, missed the tranquillity induced by the sound of surf. So, having settled in Gore, we started to explore local coastlines. Riverton felt so serene that after a weekend stay we decided to buy a property there. Naturally we meditated on the idea. The mentors said:

> The tranquillity at that location is optimal, although we enhanced it for the duration of your stay to alert you to it. Of course, the tranquility is due to its proximity to the sea. For the same reasons, Edward Cayce was counselled to find a seaside location to facilitate his spiritual work. We specify a ten kilometre distance from the sea is not too great. So anywhere on that coastline is suitable, or any other coastline, for that matter.

This was in 2017. Janet bought a crib (Southland's name for a small holiday house) near Taramea Bay in Riverton. It was rundown, so we filled the fireplace with a heat pump, upgraded the bathroom, and replaced the small rotting wooden windows with big windows on the sunny side, to enhance the sea views.

The place is serene and comfortable. The many nearby holiday houses are routinely empty, which contributes to a peaceful spiritual atmosphere.

Even when the wind blows hard, as it sometimes does, the tranquillity ensures the inner realms are usually easy to access.

On one occasion, while meditating, I noticed subtle disturbances in the local area. On examining what I was feeling, I intuited the energetic disturbance was due to the hard, marginal existence of those who settled there, and also resulted from the hunting of whales by early mariners. The result was a community-wide depressed feeling. I responded to an invitation to lift the energetic ambience, which subtly enhanced the feeling of tranquility.

This is the environment for continuing communication with the non-embodied mentors. The material that follows was predominantly received by me over the course of a year, from early 2018 to early 2019. A little material from before and after those dates has been included as appropriate.

Peter Calvert

CHAPTER ONE

—+ +—

Restating Fundamental Principles

We come into your attention to make the most of your arrival. The intention behind preparing your new retreat has been realised, this space making it possible for wisdom to be shared in optimal conditions, which we intend to do in the form of further books.

The last significant presentation of material was published as *The Kosmic Web*. We intend to extend that material here. As you are well-practised and proficient at receiving our transmissions, and what you need to do so is already in place in this new location, the settling-in period that has previously been the norm is replaced by an increase in available energy.

This is because in the interim between the last book and now a trickle of energy, intermittent yet sufficiently frequent, has sustained the quality of connection at an adequate level. But where the messages you received during the interim were in answer to diverse questions and situations, in this instance the direction is singular and for one particular purpose.

We now take your attention leftward, so you may perceive that the alternative inputs, identities and motivations that occasionally manifest from that direction are absent. This place has been declared sacrosanct. It is protected by voluminous light and is imbued with positive intention and energy to support the task in hand. Naturally, this is independent of the conditions current in your physical domain, which have deteriorated to such a degree that they may stop you from carrying out some planned activities. [It was raining heavily.] Nonetheless, the conditions are advantageous. Not that there has been any direction to control the weather, merely that the weather is focusing your attention, which suits our purpose.

Accordingly, we begin to map the task ahead, both in the immediate future, being the remaining few days before you return home, and through to the end of this project, which involves conveying specific information.

The information is not new. It builds on and, to an extent, necessarily repeats what has already been stated within the conceptual framework of this transmission. The transmission has been sustained over the last several years, with its conceptual framework having been conveyed in multiple publications, enabling it to be accessed in book form or via website content. In this introductory chapter we will summarise the extensive material already delivered, but avoid unnecessary duplication by referencing previously published material.

Accessing spiritual education

Entering the perceptual space necessary to receive this material has two preliminary requirements. The first is a receptive emotional state, in which the recipient is willing to comply with an inner request to communicate. The second is attending to the inner connection at the hara[1] level, to use terminology we have introduced elsewhere.

We emphasise the terminology is the variable. The act is what matters. Traditionally, the activity of attending within has been viewed as involving submission to what the religious term "divine will". We reject the concept of the divine, both in its customary usage and in its historical religious definition. Our intention throughout these transmissions is to redefine the relationship between the spiritual and physical, offering a description that is truer to what actually occurs.

We therefore insist, and will continue to do so throughout this short text, that our readers appreciate they possess both a lower mind and a higher mind. Further, the higher mind occupies a different space to the lower mind. Identity encompasses both minds. This means identity-level communication involves both the lower and higher minds working together.

For such communication to occur several preconditions need to be fulfilled. The recipient needs to understand that identity is dual, being located

---

[1] Hara, a Japanese term for belly. The hara dantian (from the Chinese, *tan tien*), is an energy centre two fingers below the navel. For details see *The Kosmic Web*, p 79 ff.

in both the spiritual and physical domains. When that is understood and, more importantly, detected, it becomes possible to envisage information being communicated via the hara centre. The hara centre is aligned physically with the energy centre just below the belly-button. Spiritually, it aligns with the kernel existing at each individual's spiritual centre. Hence, ultimately, the hara centre is located not in physical space but in spiritual space. As a result, transitioning through the connection at the hara centre enables curious individuals to reach into the more expansive aspects of their Self.

The Self is traditionally termed the higher self — while we use the term "higher" out of convenience, because it is in common usage, that is not literally the case. The higher self is accessed when attention transitions into the spiritual domain occupied by identity at the higher mind level. The higher mind contains the totality of information accumulated from an individual's previous incarnated identities. Hence what an enquiring individual usually encounters initially are personalities acquired during the process of constructing the higher mind. These encounters introduce the first aspects of the higher mind. We note that the concept of aspect psychology developed by the author of the Seth material[2] is relevant here.

So it is usual that prior personalities' manners, languages and cultural attributes are encountered first. However, that does depend on the extent to which they have been integrated into the higher mind, a process that commonly occurs later in the reincarnation cycle. Recognising these traits also depends on the individual being not attributing what they perceive to spirit guides. They also need to be willing to dispense with their attachment to culturally and linguistically ingrained explanations of identity. Finally, the degree to which this is achieved depends on what is commonly called the individual's "soul age". Soul age is reflected in an individual's accumulated life history, which is the sum of experiences acquired by repeatedly incarnating and experiencing multiple sub-personalities, one at a time, life after life. These conditions need to be fulfilled before entry into identity at the higher mind level becomes possible.

The accompanying graphic is an image of a partially unified Self. It il-

---

[2] Jane Roberts (1929–1984). She introduced her ideas on aspect psychology in *Adventures in Consciousness* (1975). The aspects are from other lives.

lustrates the central aspect, which contains the information procured during each life to date. It is surrounded by several information sets, gathered from prior lives, that are yet to be fully amalgamated.

This image is a good example of the inevitably over-processed nature of such depictions. It doesn't capture the Self's subtle faint pastel lilac hues, nor its transparency, nor the partial coalescence in progress, nor the quiet shining nature of the Self as it is internally perceived within shamanic space, acquired when the meditator's mind travels[3] to where it is.

The task is to integrate all the accumulated information that is uploaded to the higher mind after each life ends. This information includes each individual personality and everything they experience during the course of each life. The mature individual, who has typically lived around 600[4] lives, will have achieved a degree of integration sufficient to manifest a well-functioning higher identity. That higher identity is then available to be consulted by the individual during its current incarnation.

When that is achieved, contributions from the higher mind are available to be acted on during the current life. Generally speaking, improved direction within that life follows, resulting in outcomes that are valued both by the individuals themselves and by others, that is, when they become aware of what is occurring.

This brief description, of an identity as it functions within a life and

---

[3] Travelling by shifting the point of perception from physical through imaginal into spiritual space.

[4] This model assumes human beings experience an average of 1,000 lifetimes.

at the higher mind level, has been described throughout history numerous times. What differs here is the language used to describe it, and our denial that there is anything exceptional about this process. We emphasise that the historically supposed elevation and magnitude of the process does not require either superlatives or the concept of divinity.

Many individuals will be shocked by this declaration, that the concept of the divine is untenable and unnecessary in relation to the Self. They need not be. Factual descriptions necessarily involve removing unnecessary metaphors and sublimated meanings.

To use a common example, what distinguishes a person who can ride a bicycle and another who cannot is merely a matter of skill and control over their body's muscles. The person lacking that skill is not of lesser intrinsic worth to the person who possesses it. Similarly, to describe an identity not body-bound as intrinsically superior to one occupying a physical form is a simple error. Our task is to correct that misunderstanding.

Declaring this to be our task at the outset provides a context for all that follows. We are not alone in this. Other identities similar to ourselves are introducing these ideas and ideals into other cultures and languages as we speak. Those initiatives are not known to this identity, but a diligent search will uncover them. Where such initiatives are being undertaken within highly religious communities, the language and descriptions tend to be more circumspect, out of simple concern that the information would otherwise be regarded as heretical and thereby invite the traditional response of rejection.

This individual, having survived that type of response previously, is correspondingly cautious. It has taken many years of training, and arriving at this favourable location within this culture, to facilitate even a degree of the freedom needed to articulate these matters. Because the scars run deep.

Yet we are grateful to have at our disposal this individual and his accumulated merit, which bolster our confidence that these ideas will be transcribed accurately.

Cancelling the idea of divinity

Interest in cancelling the idea of divinity will wax and wane over the next several centuries. This is because it is different in both degree and kind from the current dominant scientific philosophical agenda, which prefers to negate all references to the reality and role of spiritual identity. Historically, the religious focus on the domain of spirit as primarily causative has resulted in as much error as today's scientific focus on the domain of the physical as the primary cause of everything. Offering a complete analysis, and a balanced conclusion, we seek to reduce over-emphasis on either.

Of course, the rhetoric associated with these topics is as much at issue as overly simplistic assumptions. Rhetoric, by definition and function, involves exercising superlatives. Superlatives are best avoided in descriptive terminology. Even the visual forms used in such discussions, such as capitals added to words of supposed significance, and vocabularies reaching towards abstruse heights of meaning, have been unsuccessful in providing a balanced evaluation of reality.

We here signal our preference is to avoid the traditional magnification of meaning, and instead adopt simple language.

Of course, the reason rhetoric is used instead of simple description is that the phenomena in question are subtle and, for the bulk of any population, invisible. Accordingly, a statistical technique, derived from an accumulation of individual empirical encounters, is the only viable way to add significantly to any discussion of intangible and invisible phenomena. Yet this requires data in relation to encounters be aggregated over time and across cultures. This, in turn, leads to certain difficulties.

As is familiar to students of Vipassana[5] meditation, anyone who retreats into the meditative state for long enough is able to register a range of sensations. These sensations generally enter the awareness because physical movement is held in check and the mind is trained to concentrate. As a consequence, meditators discover a category of pseudo-sensations attributed to the aura, which is itself a scientifically disputed phenomenon.

When enough time is spent in stillness, phenomena attributed to the aura occur sufficiently frequently that they are readily identified by the meditator. An expanded capacity to view invisible things normally follows. This results in another set of perceptions.

Unless one is meditating alone, descriptions of these sensations may

---

[5] The Buddhist meditation technique promulgated internationally by S.N. Goenka.

then be correlated with others' perceptions, clarifying what occurred, when it occurred, and to whom. First-hand experience then gives meditators a greater insight into historical descriptions of similar encounters, which they may then add to their own understanding of the phenomena they encounter. There remain two difficulties. The first is the extent to which historical descriptions may be accepted as valid. The second is allowing for exaggeration, and so adjusting expectations to match what is actually encountered.

In the context of these difficulties, a series of if-then statements may be used as part of a validation exercise. Naive explorers of their own mind and perceptual space may thus begin by saying:

If one sits for a sufficient period and attends to the subtle realm of emergent phenomena using the technique of not focussing elsewhere, *then*, in a near-random manner, a series of perceptions will arise which can be noted, described, and gradually, due to repetition, accumulate significance.

If a balanced observation technique is adopted, containing no tendency to exaggerate such perceptions nor to deny them when they occur, instead holding expectations in check and seeking to personally acquire evidence, *then* a body of experiential data will accrue.

If such accrued experiential data is then compared with that obtained by others who are similarly experienced, alert and non-judgemental, seeking to neither exaggerate, minimise nor deny such experiences, *then* the individual will find they are a member of an expanding population of such individuals.

If the recorded experiences of such individuals, meditating at other times and places, is compared with the aggregated experience over the local population, *then* similarities will be found.

If that combined experience is compared with that obtained from other eras and cultures, making a careful adjustment of terminology to allow proper translation without either exaggeration, minimisation or denial, *then* a case can be constructed in support of the reality of such phenomena.

Of course, this has been done many times. But mostly informally.

Experience, confusion, knowledge

Today, doubt concerning the occurrence and reality of these types of perceptions has penetrated to every corner of the globe. It is used to justify the stance of insensitive individuals who have not investigated, via personal exploration, any type of subtle perceptual experience. Therefore doubt has accumulated in the international mind. Just as the claim that God is dead once had a profound impact on nineteenth century Christians, today's widespread scepticism regarding spiritual phenomena has led to the widespread feeling that humanity is spiritually empty and lost.

As a result, ennui, confusion and aimlessness has multiplied. People across the planet have lost sight of their purpose for being in the world. So alternative goals of various kinds have been set up and pursued, such as accruing money and pursuing happiness. Business, sales, consumption and sensuality capture the imaginations of most populations.

There is nothing wrong with this. We claim that because the purpose for being on the planet is to gain experience, and, through appropriate processes of contemplation, to come to understand what that experience involves. In this context, every activity has value.

From the perspective of an individual's life development goals, only after they have experienced their life as a complete waste of time, mis-focussed and unsuccessful by any established parameter, are they then motivated to ensure their next life choices are made wisely.

For this reason, we consider guilt is inappropriate, it being of no more value in directing a life than any other quality. We also avoid generating yet another passionate diatribe regarding blame. We rather say that it behoves every individual to consider their life and, if they feel they need it, to seek wise counsel to do so. To the extent that they do not, then they gain the experience associated with the resulting condition. And there is nothing wrong with that, either.

In making these statements, we seek to bring order, balance and context to topics that are so easily discussed in excessive language, whether written or spoken, filled with finger-pointing and judgement, that results in confusion and depression among those who are singled out.

Neither compulsion nor loss are attached to any course of action any individual undertakes during a life. Every choice leads to an experience of some kind. And experience is what you come here to obtain.

Comparing one person to another is best avoided. Yet given the hierarchical nature of human culture, supplemented by the animal-level drive to out-compete on every level, judgement is unavoidable in this domain. Again, there is nothing wrong with this, because until an individual experiences such things how can they arrive at a balanced understanding of their worth? The astute and experienced individual will see the processes at work and choose their own objective, independent of judgements coming from those around them.

We see the confusion in the world and would prefer it be reduced. We have zero expectations that our efforts will contribute effectively to this occurring any time soon. Yet that does not forestall our attempt, nor diminish our expectation that, in coordination, we have the collective capacity to share a refreshed perspective regarding not only the nature of physical existence, but of spiritual existence and its origins.

We acknowledge all this while we attempt to make an intervention into human culture. So has every spiritual teacher throughout history. The difficulty is not intrinsically with the situation of intervening in the world — and by "world" we mean the physical domain and humanity's social life — the challenge is to be sufficiently persuasive in the face of the unstable attending of any particular embodied human, which will potentially lead to the faltering, or even failure, of our self-assigned task.

Yet an assignation between us in the non-embodied realm, and those living in the embodied realm, has been called for. This is in the literal sense that humanity as a whole, although not necessarily any particular individual, seeks a reminder so they may, while living an embodied existence, having forgotten the reality of their situation, may recall that yes, they came from somewhere else, and yes, they will return there at the end of their life.[6]

And if individuals don't immediately remember who they are and what they are here to do, then through repeated exposure to these ideas they eventually will.

---

[6] This references the traditional religious idea of salvation. See *The Matapaua Conversations* and *The Kosmic Web* for alternative views of continuity after the body dies, which show why religious exaggerations, designed to stoke fear, are invalid.

CHAPTER TWO

—✦—

Developing Spiritual Awareness

The denial that human beings are spiritual beings who possess spiritual awareness is only of concern among those who, being curious, either experience or seek to experience an indication of what spirituality entails.

Individuals for whom such sensations, perceptions and inner knowing occur naturally, and especially when these topics are commonly discussed within their family, generally have no difficulty acknowledging the existence of perceptual inputs other than the traditional six sense-doors.[1] However, after encountering those who vehemently disbelieve, deny, ridicule or misunderstand their capacities, they may retreat and begin to doubt the validity of their own experiences. Others, growing up in an opinionated climate that repudiates belief in such faculties, assuming they don't exist, may enthusiastically join in the mocking, declaring all spiritual capacities imaginary and therefore false.

Yet others may have the good fortune of growing up in a family that denies the spiritual, yet be sensitive themselves, so in their own self-interest they feel compelled to investigate their inner capacities. We offer support to this last group by affirming the following points.

Conditions for acquiring direct knowledge

The unconscious mind is commonly understood to be a feature of every person's mental cartography.[2] Adopting any of the great variety of traditional spiritual practices may be viewed as an adventure undertaken to make

---

[1] Eye, nose, tongue, ear, skin, mind.
[2] Map of mind structure and function.

known what is currently unknown but is suspected of being present at a subconscious level. For a rewarding adventure, three prerequisites are necessary: having some initial success in exploring the subconscious mind; having a supportive network of associates with whom perceptions and feelings may be shared; and having access to historical discussions regarding what is experienced when seeking to penetrate into that as yet unknown territory.

On the other hand, the life plans of many individuals, perhaps most, are not intended to do more than survive in the physical domain, and learn from managing the experience. Usually this involves raising a family, with surviving and procreating being considered enough to extract worthwhile knowledge from their life experiences.

Yet there is always a subset whose confusion and curiosity pushes them to seek a deeper understanding of their existence. They eventually come to appreciate what may potentially be gained from exploring their own mind. They may then contrast what they find with what is on record in their own and others' cultures. So the West looks East, and the East looks West, and both look backwards through time. To explore the diverse historical opinions that are available, such seekers need to travel beyond comfortable everyday perceptions. However, as already indicated, traditional descriptions of all kinds of non-everyday perceptions are contaminated by the concept of the divine. We are pleased to address this.

Many factors combine to transform the concept of the divine into an almost impassable minefield. Historically, these factors have invariably been religious. They include extreme idealisation, over-stated attributions, ignorant misunderstanding, and deliberately false representations of real contributions to humanity's spiritual well-being. Particularly harmful are repeated descriptions of the divine as perfect and the physical as limiting and even evil, which perpetuates self-doubt and low self-esteem. Together, these factors generate misapprehensions and misinterpretations of all kinds.

We aim to bring order and simplicity to this confusing minefield. Accordingly, we will outline a model of human identity, and its functioning in embodied existence, by discussing patterns of relationships and their destination. These patterns will appear familiar to some, and outlandish to others. Nevertheless, we begin by offering a description of the fundamentals of reality.

The physical and the spiritual

We first bifurcate reality into physical space and spiritual space. Physical space is so well known we need not describe it further. Instead, we will focus on spiritual space, and on the dynamics of interchange between spiritual space and physical space.

It is first necessary to appreciate that these two spaces, these two domains, interpenetrate. Historically, attempts have been made to establish a hierarchical relationship between the two. In this discussion, we will ignore them. The two are co-existing aspects of one continuum.

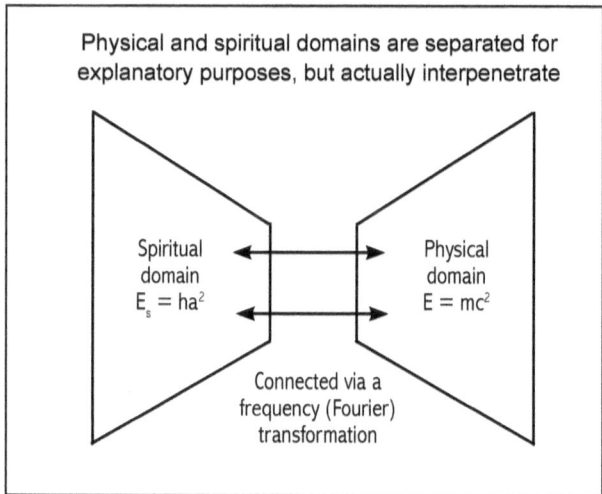

Our description begins with the contention that identity arises spontaneously within spiritual space.[3]

After consciousness comes awareness of self-identity.

That is followed by encounters with other identities similar to oneself, which leads to a sense of community. Exchanges of information at the community level creates awareness that opportunities are available. Specifically, opportunities to acquire knowledge, and in the process to extend one's individual skills and capabilities in desirable ways.

---

[3] For more detail see Appendix: Nodes of Dao-Consciousness.

Those who are bold consequently enter the physical domain, where they are wrapped in a dense perceptual veil. They do so to co-associate with one or other physical creature. Their purpose is to encounter myriad opportunities, to accumulate experiences from which they learn, to extract information from what they learn, and to develop their personal faculties and capacities. Thus in this particular nook of the universe they make use of the opportunity to co-associate with the species that calls itself Homo sapiens sapiens. Or, more commonly, humanity.

Humanity is neither special nor blessed, to use those traditional but inappropriate terms. Rather, humanity is just another of innumerable species that are self-aware, comparatively intelligent, and that offer opportunities to experience, learn and develop. We won't discuss other species here as they lie outside the scope of this discussion.

Readers will be aware that in presenting a narrative of origins in this way we have declined to include any reference to the traditional hierarchical relationship of human beings to God. That is simply because no evidence supports such an idea. Hence referring to it will not help those who seek deep understanding.

We are well aware that among various groups our declining to include a relationship of humanity to God will automatically lead to our description being rejected. But it is not our agenda to support such a distinction. Nor do we wish to argue against it, simply because culturally it has crytallised beyond recovery.

Our perspective is that a spiritual individual co-associates with a physical individual, and chooses to maintain their association until the body dies. They then return to their point of focus in spiritual space, which they in fact occupied all along. The journey into and out of physicality is that simple.

From the perspective of the spiritual identity who occupies a human body, that the experience is not easy, and often fraught, is of no consequence. This is because as soon as the spiritual identity permanently disassociates from the physical form it co-associated with, it regains its prior understanding. Those who appreciate this before their body's demise make the transition from the physical domain to the spiritual domain with less difficulty, because of their greater innate acceptance.

More could be added to this description of the arc identities follow as they penetrate the dense veil of physicality, then return to the spiritual realm. Conversely, much has already been said.

One point we wish to emphasise is that long-established concerns regarding the role the so-called divine will plays in an individual's journey from the spiritual to the physical and back again, and the heartfelt longing embodied human beings have to live in the supposedly superior heavenly world, and the widely shared fear that they may not be admitted there after their body dies — all these feelings are inappropriate.

The journey happens, life after life after life. The process is best understood in the simplest possible way. There is certainly no need for fear or guilt, nor for confusion or reluctance, nor for all the other mental, emotional and physical barriers that unnecessarily burden individuals as they journey between the spiritual and physical domains.

All who read this are currently co-associating with a body. When your body dies you will cease to do so. You will then return to full awareness of your identity residing in the spiritual realm. After a period of absorbing what has been experienced and learned, you will select another body to co-associate with. You will live another life, in which you will experience and learn. Nothing divine is involved. Being human is that easy. And, given the complexities of human existence, that difficult.

Untaught knowing

If you know something it is because you have a history that connects you to it. This leads us to discuss untaught knowing.

Untaught knowing occurs when you feel, think or do this or that without having been told about it or read about it. The current contemporary view is that such occurrences are inexplicable mysteries. This is due to the widespread unwillingness to acknowledge that something can be known as a result of what has been experienced previously, while occupying a body prior to one's current body.

We offer an alternative view, pointing to untaught knowing as evidence that supports ancient understanding, which is that you occupy a series of bodies and accumulate experience and information from each. When a life is completed that information is stored at the higher self level. An experience of untaught knowing occurs when an individual accesses the understanding stored at their higher self level and transfers it into their awareness at the everyday level of their current embodied identity.

To explain the difference in the simplest terms, those who experience untaught knowing have access to their higher self, whereas those who don't do not.

Accessing the higher self is the mark of a maturing soul, to use that terminology. So when a young person is asked, "How do you know that?", and, confused, they respond, "I don't know where I learned it. I just knew!", it is appropriate to support them. Such people are likely to become competent in unexpected ways, enjoying a life path that takes them beyond the circumstances that otherwise limit members of the family they were born into.

To conclude this brief disquisition, untaught knowing is a reliable indicator of future capability.

Union with one of this transmission's two sources

To continue this discussion, we project our identity and ideas into this physical domain, which you call yours. It is also ours, because we have been there. It is not where we now reside, as all the identities of which we are constituted have concluded their rounds of lives and reunified at the spiritual level.

The argument could be made that because our occupancy on this planet has ended our perspective is no better than that of any embodied person. Against this we observe that we take as our purview the current state of world affairs, as well as all the planet's inhabitants, past and present.

Having, in that respect, inspected this individual [Peter], we recognise that given the choices we have among those who could function as an amanuensis, he is as good as any and better than most. Our choice is not without a cost to him, as he has been involved in many years of training in order to nullify personality-led voyeurism, vices and inclinations. This is because we recognise the risks of exciting animosity among others, as well as of personal traits such as self-will, egocentric bias and a desire for cult formation, all of which we have declined to stimulate. History attests that in other places and eras those personality traits have led to significant deviations from what was communicated.

Accordingly, we have fostered both autonomy and dependence in our relationship. By agreement, our relationship continues. However, we remain cautious, given there is always a risk of stirring false or questionable claims regarding the authenticity of these communications. In that regard, this individual's passive nature is an asset that is among his best qualities. Cultivating his passivity has involved him in exploring past experiences, bringing to light resulting tendencies, and reducing or eliminating their impact via salutary lessons. That so much has been achieved gives us confidence our relationship will remain more positive than otherwise.

Now the reason for our presence with you today.

Sunshine on the closed eyelids [indirectly refracted through a coarse cotton curtain] suitably represents our domain of existence. Suffused by a golden light and a serene goodwill, we fit traditional descriptions, because in this case they are not wrong.

[Peter has closed his eyes and is enveloped by a deep tranquillity.]

Now you are within us, perceive the tranquillity. On the previous occasion you had an experience like this you interpreted it to be due to the presence of Guan Yin.[4] There is only one Guan Yin. We are not it. Yet the quality of lower mind being immersed in the higher identity is similar. As is being absorbed into a benign, non-judgemental, loving, inclusive presence.

This experience may be termed a state of grace. But that traditional term is insufficient, because it connotes divinity. We say, extract divinity and union remains.

It is rare, certainly. It is memorable, certainly. It involves experiencing ecstasy, certainly. There is nurture. There is positive regard. There is willingness to support. There is absence of time to constrain nurture and support. To that degree, eternity is a valid descriptor where divinity is not.

Psychologically, it accepts every aspect and tendency, acted on or not. It accepts self and shadow in every life endured, proclaimed or denied.

In this state no reprimand is possible. There is only infinite goodwill. The term "infinite" signifies no limit in either time or degree.

---

[4] A Chinese Buddhist name for the bodhisattva associated with compassion. Guanyin is short for Guanshiyin, which means "The one who perceives the sounds of the world". This references how she is always listening to people suffering and crying out for help, ready to go to their aid.

This state exudes compassion for the likely impacts of each life plan. And respect for the boldness required to willingly embark on a journey into the tempestuous conflict endemic in human existence.

This state of union is a rare experience for the embodied human being who is inevitably battered by the feelings of acceptance and rejection inherent in primal, competitive, reactive embodied life.

Yet this state is not special. It is echoed in the affection a mother feels for her newborn child. This state is encountered in utero if the mother is living in low stress circumstances. However, it is rarely encountered thereafter, unless replicated in a very positive maternal relationship, or in a loving partnership. The need for the adult human to remain alert to external threats means it is seldom experienced unaided. Which is fitting, because externally directed attention aids survival in the physical domain.

This state of union is dependent on facilitating conditions, in this case being isolated, being conditioned by a few days of preparation, being protected by safe enclosure, and being supported by the necessities for survival, well-rested, in no need of anything. Beyond these conditions, this sense of being at the centre and surrounded by love has become available by special arrangement.

The rarity of this state is the primary reason people associate it with divinity. Where there is hunger for this state of union, the idea it involves divinity becomes supremely attractive, due to the contrast between it and the normally fraught conditions of human existence. It is quite understandable that the promise of union with magnitude triggers a hunger to experience it.

So superlatives are used, because no other words sufficiently describe the difference between such a state and the demands of ordinary life and its common emotional spectrum. Yet superlatives are not justified if they are utilised to advertise. Superlatives are only valid if they are used to describe. They then accurately illustrate the difference between the emotional spectrum of ordinary life and the emotional spectrum of the tranquil, loving, accepting state of union.

If one thinks of the spectrum of emotion laid out as a topographic surface, then this state is a prominent impulse, glowing with love, rising up above all the surrounding emotions like a bright gold column or spire.

With this experience complete, we withdraw.

[From Peter's journal]

One could summarise that experience as comprising the bliss of union. A singular experience. Very special. It's funny, the sunlight now looks dim and wan, distinctly lacking that feeling of brightly shining gold. No wonder gold metal is highly valued. Goodness me, that's forty-three minutes. That's very similar to the Guan Yin experience. I'm a bit reluctant to let go of it. It's definitely made my day!

Questions about divinity

I formulated the following questions as a response to the experience of union with the reunited, reintegrated node of Dao-consciousness:

1. What is the role of experience such as yesterday's in the formation of the concept of divinity?
2. Who was the original creator of that concept?
3. How did it come to be the default position?
4. What difficulties did it solve so as to become so entrenched a belief?
5. Why is it wrong?
6. Why is it now unnecessary?
7. How can it be repealed as the most favoured concept?
8. What can be done to enable that?
9. By whom is such action best performed?
10. Where will resistance arise?
11. How best to present the argument and to whom?
12. Is presentation via the proposed book sufficient?
13. If not, what else?
14. Does it matter?
15. Given the investment in the concept of divinity throughout international religious thought, is it a futile project?
16. How might it be funded, and why?
17. What are the logical consequences?
18. Are they valid?

19. Or likely?
20. Given that every mother offers the experience of unconditional love to their newborn child, what psychological factors can explain its reification to ultimacy, in the religious sense, in the adult?
21. Is it a phenomenon of male power, loss and yearning for a return to the breast?
22. Or is such psychological postulation unnecessary?
23. If so, what else has conditioned the concept and fuelled its universality?
24. Given that I have now met and experienced the bliss of absorption from two reunited reintegrated identities each comprising about a million individual lifetimes of experience, have felt that state to be desirable, yet am willing to deny the experience as unification with God, where is God if not there?
25. Is there even such a thing/phenomenon/identity as God?
26. Or is it all a case of mistaken attribution of identity?
27. Is it attributable to the necessity to strengthen the intrinsically weak case for spiritual experience in the face of the palpable experience of physical reality? To this question I received a resounding inner, "Yes!"
28. How does the mussel farm model of spiritual identity help this clarification and discussion?
29. How to map this whole discussion?

[Next morning the mentors responded:] The answers will be forthcoming in the coming days and weeks. Meanwhile return home. Your work is done here for now.

CHAPTER THREE

Spirituality, Religion, Science

[From Peter's journal]
I have been reviewing my questions and realised that the only response so far was to Q27, concerning whether the concept of divinity is based on the necessary reification[1] of spiritual experience, because of the intrinsically weak case made for spiritual experience given humanity is normally so entranced by palpable physical life. And, I guess, by the emotionality of the body.

We have been waiting for you to recognise that this is the only significant question. All the others can be dispensed with, because even though it is appropriate that they be asked, reaching as they do into many dimensions of human life, the only significant portion is the reference contained in Q27 to the faint, fleeting and therefore ephemeral nature of most spiritual experiences.

Such experiences are in fact common. That is their power. But in some instances an individual who has such an experience feels so elevated by it that they describe it to others, which leads to their experience gaining significance by virtue of it being culturally amplified. The social impact is so strong that the experiencing individuals are given an elevated status.

---

[1] *Reify*, verb, to make something abstract more concrete or real. Religions originate in ephemeral spiritual experiences. To make these experiences more "concrete" and "real" later followers create physically enacted rituals to echo them and doctrines to explain them. Over time, as exegesis is added to doctrines, then exegesis to the exegesis, worshippers' attention is displaced further and further from their religion's original ephemeral experiences. This is how religions reify their founders' spiritual experiences.

Despite this type of social response, such ephemeral spiritual experiences are significant. That is because they often address, or at least hint at, a larger picture, which is that the answers to fundamental questions regarding human existence lie just "over the horizon" of space and time. When others validate this via their own experiences, then the reputation of that class of ephemeral experience is enhanced.

The reason is they are literally out of the ordinary. By which we mean they are obtained without the mediation of the senses, in the conventional meaning of that term.

Sciences and spiritual experience

That said, we continue our dialogue. We wish to bring a necessary balance to our argument regarding individuals' desire to seek spiritual experience by drawing attention to the achievements of science. Scientific discoveries and theories offer explanations of existence and origins that are as significant as any ancient religious formulation. If not more so, given that, in many instances, explanations offered by the sciences are orders of magnitude more profound than those offered in historical religious texts.

It is no accident this is the case, because the accumulated knowledge contained within the data collected by modern sciences dwarfs the traditional expressions of belief promulgated by today's religions. This does not reduce the significance of religion for anyone interested in human origins and history. But it most assuredly does render the religious understanding of existence and origins comparatively insignificant when contrasted to the knowledge accumulated through the systematic application of the scientific method to numerous fields of study. Therefore, there is nothing wrong with any individual who simply chooses to follow the scientific path of understanding and ignore religious history.

This will be difficult to accept by individuals trained to defer to the founts of wisdom expounded by their exemplars, by which we mean the prophets of this planet's religions. Indeed, individuals indoctrinated while children into a religious tradition, and having been programmed to accept ideals taught by their religious teachers, would object that our previous statement is a great heresy.

We merely respond that is not the case. Because if later doctrinal elaborations are extracted from any religious tradition, and the tradition is reduced to its originating actuality, which is a history of faint and ephemeral impressions, and those ephemeral impressions are placed alongside the data-sets accumulated in any field of scientific enquiry, they will be seen to be lesser by orders of magnitude.

Accordingly, in our opinion this provides the basis for a fundamental rebalancing of what contemporary humanity considers significant. Specifically, it is our view that the significance assigned to traditional religious teachings should be rejected. Religious teachings are not special. They are culturally specific, consisting of statements made in particular eras, to particular groups of people, utilising particular conceptual frameworks, constructed on the basis of what was then known, and more often supposed, about the world and those living in it.

We come into this domain to provide a reference point, from which we proclaim — while conscious that we are, ironically, following the traditional religious pattern — that traditional religious understanding has been elaborated beyond reason. We propose such elaboration be undone, and that each religious teaching be consigned to its period in history and allowed to rest there, neither denied nor forgotten, but accepted as examples of the age-old human propensity to have precious, ephemeral experiences. As such, historical religions will be appreciated as providing now out-moded models of what is of ultimate significance to human beings. That said, we rest our case.

The argument against religion

[Transcribed from Peter's recording of a meditation session]
Scanning my immediate zone of shamanic space, I identify something at forward left 30 degrees, slightly up 5 degrees. Otherwise the perceptual volume around me seems empty. I sense now that the presence consists of a cluster of individuals. I invite them closer, seeking dialogue. Why have you come?

They've come closer. I get the feeling of pugnaciousness. They're muscular, aggrieved, sad, wanting to avenge false accusations, murder, the stealthy dispossession of their lands. I sense arguments against the dominant forces of culture, religion and power that marginalised them, condemning them as misfits adhering to aberrant beliefs, and so targeting and ridiculing them, depriving them of justice. They rail against human nature, which seeks to take advantage of them at every turn. They have been over-run by wars, displaced from their lands, forced to trudge in retreat from conflict zones, unable to return.

I say to them: This is not the fault of religion so much as of humanity. Any argument in support of power is deceptive, at best. You have incarnated to encounter your fellow man's ugliness and decline to participate in it. Go in peace to the light now, where your history will be understood and your humanity enhanced.

They move into the light. This group gave the impression that they were Middle-Eastern people, perhaps Kurdish, Iranian, or similar.

I sense another presence, forward 30 degrees, 60 degrees down, left side. I invite it up to this level. I get the impression of animated gesticulation, that these are a group of agitated women who feel they have been consigned to the wrong place and now seek repatriation, compensation, restoration.

I say to them: Understand your condition. Your rights on Earth and among its population are extinguished now. The only destination now is the light. Quiet your concerns. Open your perception and look. See the light and as a group move to it quickly, shepherding all with you.

They are gone. I sensed they were Muslim women wearing hijab, displaced from life by war.

We come to you now to discuss what results when one group imposes their religious beliefs on another.

While traditional religious injunctions promote equality and love for all, throughout history the human animal's desire to dominate and impose hierarchy has always functioned in opposition to universal justice. The unholy alliance, as it has often been called, of power, authority and conquest, frees one group to project its influence over another groups' territory, to the detriment of the invaded population.

Tribalism and symbols, effectively forms of advertising, have historically been used to indoctrinate and motivate populaces in order to unify them against those their leaders have chosen to invade, exploit or oppress. That a local god is commonly also invoked, and its blessing claimed, is merely part of the symbology. Simply, all such tribal aggression may be categorised as humanity competing with itself.

Those who adopt a universal, equitable, detached view always abhor such savagery. Yet they understand that this planet, like every other planet populated by competing identities, provides a crucible for development, in which the incarnated discover the value of justice by experiencing its opposite. The experience of injustice is multifaceted. It includes taking part in unjust actions, suffering from unjust actions, avenging unjust actions, forgiving unjust actions, seeking reparation for unjust actions, and helping others process and forgive themselves and others for initiating, passively witnessing, or being unable to save others from injustice.

So, in the broadest sense, nothing wrong is taking place when injustice occurs, because these are the travails through which incarnating individuals gain progressively deeper understanding. Religions, for all their faults, are merely puppets in that play.

> [From Peter's journal]
> The previous argument against religion has left me feeling heavy, as if infected and burdened with the woe generated by war. So I offer a prayer.
>
> I ask that all those not yet returned to light because they are weighed down by the impact of war, with all its turmoil and injustice, terror and torture, be released to the light.
>
> I ask that they be helped to rise up from their place, wherever they are, in darkness and isolation, self-imposed or otherwise, whether hiding out of fear or because they were pursued.
>
> I ask that opposed sides come together and see their shared humanity as greater than their differences, territorial or whatever else. And that in the hiding places they have fabricated they

will now sense there is an opportunity to dismantle those dark places and see on the horizon the light that can release them.

I ask that they find themselves in the company of those who, like them, have been enslaved, confined, and reduced as persons to the lowest common denominator, whatever their personal situation may have been before they succumbed to the dissolution of their flesh.

I ask that, again finding themselves whole and together, their identity and purpose restored, they now make their way home to the light, collecting and encouraging each other along the way. May they all be at peace.

CHAPTER FOUR

Origin of the Swastika

[From Peter's journal]
Having arrived in Riverton, eaten and drunk two cups of coffee this afternoon, and having just finished my last of the day, I decided to sit in meditation.

After a short time I felt my attention go far to the right, on the same level or a little up, maybe 5 to 10 degrees. I then received the query, "Are you ready?" Thinking it was an introduction to these several days, rather than meaning "Are you ready now?", I said yes.

I immediately gained imagery of the way the Earth moves through physical space as part of its rotation around the sun, and beyond that the Sun's movement within the spiral arms of the galaxy, resulting in the realisation that our planet performs a convoluted twisting motion through interstellar space.

Two weeks ago I drew a cross. Its esoteric origin, which I noted at the time with references, is that the physical plane is represented by the horizontal bar and the spiritual plane by the vertical bar. I now realise my vision offers a simple explanation for the swastika symbol. Because if the cross is spun, then one can imagine its momentary location in the present, subdivided into the cross formation, representing the physical and spiritual planes. A spiral motion is created by the movement of those dimensions, through not only the plane of the ecliptic at the solar level, but throughout space-time.

I see that as a simple explanation for the swastika's shape

and symbol, recognised in the far distant past, and again now. The rotation could be either clockwise or anti-clockwise, depending on one's alignment and motion in relation to a chosen particular reference point.

I subsequently sought clarification in meditation: I have previously requested text to describe the origin, construction and context for the image of the swastika, situating a person living on the surface of the planet, experiencing the planet's trajectory and rotation. It occurs to me it deserves describing in the general case, beyond this planet, which presumably is a special case.

The cross and the swastika

Your realisations so far support the general understanding that where an individual takes a body, and occupies it for some time, they necessarily experience planetary rotation, resulting from the planet's orbit around the local star, the movement of that star within the galaxy it occupies, and the movement of the galaxy within the universe. That general case may be understood through the particular case of an individual on this planet, which is who we are addressing.

This particular instance of the general case is necessarily factored into our description of life on this planet, which is that bodies grow while co-associating with an in-dwelling spirit. On various occasions throughout history sensitive individuals have found their understanding stretched by feeling as if they were tumbling through space. In this way they experienced rotation, a form of instruction that led them to conclude there is a physical world and also a spiritual world. These two worlds can be conceived as occupying complementary planes, cleaving to one another, with a ninety degree orientation or displacement between them.

That is the origin of the understanding that lead to the emblem of the cross being created. As a symbol, it has historically been adopted by various religions, as well as during Christianity's emergence.

There are multiple precedents for doing so. Earlier examples have been identified in a variety of locations, East and West. Rotation has been indicated in several ways, the simplest of which is to draw a trail at the tip, intended to remind observers that yes, there is a slow rotation of the pair of planes. As happens to such things, the illustration was codified, examples of which have become memes in their own right, associated with different religions in different eras. The symbol has also been incorporated into decorative patterns on fabric and in other media. Over time, it has become disconnected from its origins.

Accordingly, we take this opportunity to affirm once again the fact of the symbol's ancient origins, of its grounding in ancient understanding, which we now supplement with a fresh explanation, adding to its traditional esoteric meaning its physical meaning in relation to the fields of astronomy and cosmology. We also note a fundamental error in this conceptualisation.

A long-standing error

The primary error, of course, is that the intention to illustrate the existence of both the physical and spiritual domains of existence has resulted in a pair of lines being drawn at ninety degrees to each other. This is false.

The physical horizon is the obvious origin for the horizontal line. The second line's orientation, at right angles and proceeding into the sky, derives from people's frequent experience that spiritual movement has a vertical dimension. This is the origin of the idea that spiritual communicants are displaced in the vertical direction.

Unfortunately, this idea has had a number of disadvantageous consequences, which we intend to both unpack and demote by offering a more detailed understanding.

What contaminates the relationship between non-embodied spiritual communicants and embodied recipients is that recipients tend to perceive communications as arriving from a forwards and upwards quadrant, relative to them. Historically, this perception has been coupled to the hierarchical relationships natural to this planet's animal species, which adopt postures of dominance or submissiveness. With recipients perceiving communications as coming from forwards and above, they have then tended to interpret them as superior, and so have adopted an attitude of submission

We take this opportunity to declare that none of this is appropriate. Every such communication is with a spiritual identity, who is best viewed as spiritually equal to the recipient. By stating this, we seek to decontaminate all the suggestions of relative value traditionally assigned to the mystic in relation to their God. The primary contaminant being the word "god".

It is much more appropriate to view every such communication as being between one identity occupying the spiritual domain and another identity also occupying the spiritual domain, but who happens to be co-associating with a physical form. There is no need to ascribe inequality to their relationship. The difference between them is merely that the identity who is physically embodied is tumbling through space, their movement determined by the rates of rotation of their planet, of their planet around its star, and by the star's rotation around the centre of its galaxy. Whereas the non-embodied spiritual identity does not do so.

This, then, can be invoked as a primary distinction between an embodied spiritual identity and any non-embodied spiritual identity. The speed of such movement, even when in the hundreds of kilometers per second range, as is common, is no impediment to ongoing proximity and communication between embodied and non-embodied identities. The intention to reach out to one another in order to communicate is sufficient.

Peter: Well, that's different from what I expected. And clearer.

Detaching historical usage from 21st century usage

Given there is a simple and factual basis for the formation and historical application of the swastika symbol, as it is known in European culture, it may justifiably be separated from its utilisation by the National Socialist German Worker's Party, commonly called the Nazi Party.

We note that last century the swastika became associated with eugenics, which created a dark chapter in human cultural history. Recent analysis of ancient DNA has clarified humanity's genetic origins, and how genes mixed through time. This has demolished the concept of racial purity, thereby making impossible the continuance of the Nazi eugenic fallacy, except in the rhetoric from current ambitious and ignorant would-be leaders in various country's alt.right movements.

Human adaptation to living in the northern hemisphere led to a reduction in melanin production, which in turn led to increased skin transparency and greater vitamin D synthesis within the skin. That quite recent adaptation is a simple product of genetic adaptation to the local environment. Yet it has generated a series of cultures that have equated greater whiteness with greater value. This conflation is inappropriately given elevated social status. The idea of cultural superiority based on skin colour is another fallacy we do not support.

Individuals exist by virtue of the incoming spiritual identity, carrying its accumulated personal history, co-associating with a newborn infant. From the perspective of the indwelling spirit the body's characteristics have only utilitarian value. That an individual, at their local mind level, subsequently uses bodily characteristics to obtain social advantage is a common human strategy. But it is a mistake. It signals a refusal to treat all other ensouled human beings, and individuals in every other species, as equals.

We belabour this point in a likely futile attempt to assert, once again, the universal equality, at the level of spiritual identity, of all incarnate life. We emphasise this point in an attempt to bring clarity to the current shock, stoppages and cross-cultural gatherings[1] of individuals identifying with brown as a shade of black, or black people themselves, and assert this simple recognition: that each person is best considered equal to every other.

The persistence of intercultural racist rhetoric and antisocial attitudes is a blight on humanity. People of goodwill and balanced thinking already know this. We provide an update from a perspective of spiritual identity in order to drive home that humanity needs to recognise that cultural superiority claimed by one indigenous class and population over any other is simply the politics of power. We abhor this.

On the other hand, the politics of love is unequivocal in its recognition and promotion of the law, which acknowledges everyone is equal. Social privilege is an embarrassment, even though natural to the human animal.

That contrast reveals the dichotomy at work in intercultural conflicts grounded in hierarchies of value. This recognition leaves it a matter of simple choice for every individual. Do they choose to act from belief in their identity as comprising nothing more important than their local mind personality and its animal body, succumbing to the natural social proclivities

---

[1] In reference to 2020's worldwide Black Lives Matter protests..

of engaging in power and one-upmanship? Or do they choose to give more importance to the principle of equality, as exists at the level of their spiritual identity and its higher mind?

There is no single answer to this dilemma. It is a matter of each person's free choice. Within those choices lie possibilities for karma production and reduction, for pursuing a life plan, and for enhancing allegiance based on knowledge of one's spiritual identity. Or, alternatively, to choose satisfaction by foregoing all these to focus on accruing maximum advantage for oneself as an individual embodied human, and so choosing to ignore all spiritual rhetoric.

It may be validly argued that the latter choice is perfectly functional. It creates the experience those individuals desire, for which they entered a body. Ultimately, we take no moral position on the desirability of making either choice. Clearly understanding what one is choosing, and the consequences of that choice, is a desired outcome of every life.

CHAPTER FIVE

A Universal Model of Existence

[From Peter's journal]
This is an experiment in posture in order to comfortably and reliably use the phone to record. I'm sitting in the big armchair at Riverton. I was up and dressed at first light, and have enjoyed the new LED light in the little kitchen. I like the light quality much better than the 60 watt incandescent lamp. I spent time today transcribing earlier recordings, have gone for a walk on the beach, and after returning had a glass of wine before beginning meditation.

We observe that the circumstances are optimal, the opportunity benign, and the posture adequate. The computer has a technical difficulty, therefore we absolve you of responsibility for transcribing between dictations.

Imbibing wine is a useful ploy. It segregates ordinary beach time, marking a shift to a different type of time. Or, at least, a period in which the purpose is not relaxation, although relaxation is a necessary preliminary, of course. Our intended purpose is rather to commune, communicate and console.

The result is, as your new colleague Michael Sosteric defines it, a connection event. We approve of that language and will utilise it. The connection is nothing other than lower mind connecting to higher mind. Sosteric's attachment to traditional terminology will be easily dissuaded. He is in our employ, to use that phrase.

---

[1] M. Sosteric, *Everybody has a connection experience.* https://athabascau.academia.edu/DrS

Your discovery of his work is not random, but has been facilitated by us. He has the credentials you do not. He has done at least as much work as you have. The range of factors he can illuminate are greater than yours. And there is nothing wrong with that.

Into these two minds we bring harmony. We refer to the harmony coexisting between higher mind and lower mind when they are connected, and equally between lower minds when connected in a common purpose. His purpose is essentially in common with yours and ours, as with Keith Hill. So we now have a triumvirate of a different kind. We celebrate that.

Instructions for the model's development

We move on now to the purpose of bringing you here. Various factors are in play that, taken together, will contribute to a new initiative in relation to communicating this perspective in a manner that will appear reasonable and attractive to erudite readers. We do not concern ourselves with those who do not categorise themselves as erudite, or who are categorised by others as less than erudite.

We ask readers not to misinterpret this claim. Ours is not a strategy promoting class. Ours is a strategy of speaking to decision-makers, speaking to opinion-makers, and speaking to those with sufficient breadth of understanding that they may easily interpret what we intend to say, which we add to what we have already said.

We are addressing those who have the mental flexibility to easily and comfortably shift between the parameters of field and interpretive boundary, to demarcate and differentiate between those factors, to shift frames of reference, to understand the distinction between one frame of reference and another, and to track the implications of shifts in frames of reference, without becoming confused. We desire nothing other than to communicate with those able to follow our descriptions.

We are aware our intent may easily be interpreted as other than that, but unreservedly deny it.

To briefly summarise what we have already provided before we extend this discussion of the nature of human existence:

- Categorisation of the boundary between the spiritual and physical domains has been dealt with at length. Using the descriptions of electrophysical, electromagnetic, electrospiritual and purely spiritual is sufficient as set of metaphors to describe domain boundaries.[2]
- The quality of existence in the different domains has been well mapped. The set of metaphoric models transferred so far, via the agapéic space model, which differentiates one sub-domain from another, is now complete.[3]

Our intention now is to provide more clarity about the way the agapéic space model is located within the ultimate unmanifest, as we are electing to identify it. This is required because the idea remains extremely vague. The difficulty arises due to trying to identify, within the ultimate unmanifest, which is formless and infinite, where human beings may situate themselves, and illutrate it using standard perspective.

To create such an illustration, we begin by suggesting you, our reader, picture a vast unbounded space. Imagine that within this space is an occupiable volume, which contains all that is ordinarily termed "existence". And that this vastness, which extends infinitely in at least three dimensions, contains a domain that may be mapped using the measuring tools of physical science. This material domain — we use the term "material" advisedly — facilitates the potential existence of physical universes. One of those universes is this universe, in which you, our reader, and this book you are reading, exist. By extension, you may now appreciate, conceptually, there is a place for humanity in the map, within the universe as humanity currently understands it.

Being able to offer such a perspective, however ephemeral it is in relation to the solidness of ordinary existence, is important. It relates to the credibility of what we are seeking to explain. We will come back to this shortly. Right now we return to the issue of visually modelling the universe.

Having established boundaries and a perspectival view, the next step is clarifying whether the construct can be viewed from a variety of directions. In fact, at the scale we are discussing, which is of an infinite space that encloses a universe, which human beings effectively experience as boundless

---

[2] See *The Kosmic Web*, pp 79–84.
[3] See *The Kosmic Web*, pp 105–123 and *Learning Who You Are* pp 76–89.

and infinite, notional directions are impractical. Instead, we refer to an illustrative experience given previously. This is a multiverse model, which depicts a number of physical universes in relation to the *observer*.[4]

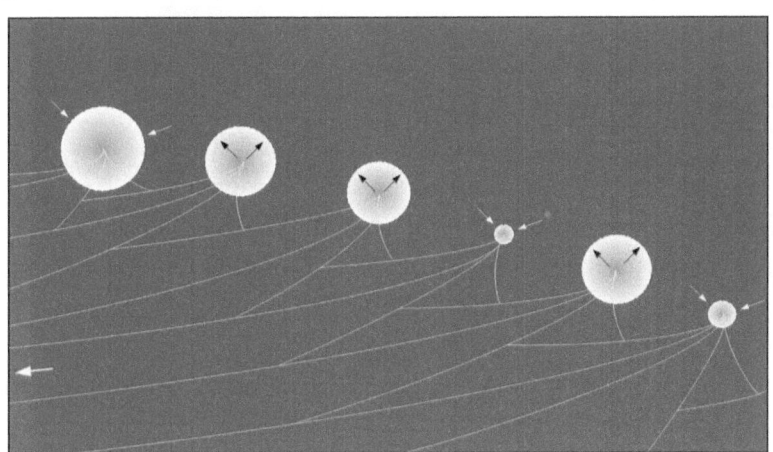

This sketch is based on a spontaneous vision Peter had in 2012. The uniform background is the featureless unmanifest and the spheres are the manifest multiple universes asynchronously and repeatedly expanding and contracting at their individual rate. That rate was perceived as approximately 1 to 3 seconds. Each universe manifested a similar maximum diameter before collapsing again. The web represents the tethering process of sustained intention to the *observer* in this experiment in the field of existence. The *observer* is the impersonal, desireless intent of the Dao, the ultimate unmanifest. The *observer* was not observed but was known to be there. The individual universes seemed somehow tethered to the edge of the viewing field, equidistant in a radial arc from the locus of perception by the *observer*.

This illustration is sufficient for our purpose here, due to the impossibility of creating another conceptual framework via which to locate relations between one universe and another. Every emergent species has its reference point, within their universe, that they use to map local space and the star system of which they are a part. Naturally, no embodied species can physically map, measure or establish location in any universe outside their own. Relations between universes can only be understood conceptually.

---

[4] This is a vision given to Peter. See *The Matapaua Conversations*, p 20 ff.

Every emergent civilisation, then, maps their local space. If there is no overlap between one species' spatial map of their universe and a different species' spatial map of the same universe, that is of no consequence. Unless, of course, there is communication between them, which gives them the opportunity to meet. We note that individual human beings have met individuals of other species from other worlds within this universe and, less commonly, from other universes.

However, humanity currently uses maps that demarcate location in physical space only. It has no maps that identify location in electromagnetic space, electrospiritual space, or agapéic space. Nor does humanity have either a conceptual framework or a vocabulary for articulating the nature of those meetings. Hence such meetings currently remain "off the reservation", as is said. They cannot be described in contemporary human terms.

That is why new maps are necessary. Yet, in saying "new" we are aware that they cannot be "too new". That is, they cannot shift so far from what human beings currently experience and understand that they become unintelligible. That is why we presented the illustration of the multiverse in the way we did. It is beyond current scientific descriptions, but only a step beyond, so we expect most readers who have reached this point will have no great difficulty understanding what we intend. Whether any of our readers accepts it is, of course, another matter.

That said, we continue by offering yet another model of existence. It is the ancient Indian metaphor of Indra's net.

Rethinking Indra's net

Ideas regarding Indra's net have been contaminated by centuries of interpretative errors. Today it is interpreted physically, with respect to weather and climate change.[5] We wish to assert the legitimacy of its original usage. Specifically, we wish to assert its legitimacy by relating it to the vision recorded

---

[5] For example, Stephanie Kaza's *Green Buddhism: Practice and Compassionate Action in Uncertain Times* (2019) discusses Indra's net in relation to climate change. A short story by Professor Vandana Singh, *Indra's Web*, uses it in relation to human harm to ecological systems as well as climate change, linking ancient Indian mythology to future technological solutions.

Indra's net: a summary

The metaphor of Indra's net first appears in the *Atharva Veda*, dating to around 1100 BCE. In ancient Indian mythology, Indra was the ruler of the gods. In the *Artharva Veda* Indra's net is described as being hung over his palace on the peak of Mount Meru and extending infinitely in all directions. A pragmatic warrior, Indra used it to capture his enemies:

"Vast indeed is the tactical net of great Indra, mighty of action and tempestuous of great speed. By that net, O Indra, pounce on all the enemies that none escape arrest and punishment." — *Artharva Veda*, verse 8.8.6 [6]

The image of Indra's net was subsequently adapted into a philosophic metaphor in a Buddhist text, *Avatamsaka Sutra* (*Flower Garland* or *Flower Ornament Sutra*), where it is used metaphysically to describe the heavenly realms. The sutra was originally written in Sanskrit between the 1st and 4th centuries. It was translated into Chinese in the 5th and 7th centuries, which both preserved it and elaborated on it. The English translation by Thomas Cleary runs to over 1600 pages.

The metaphor of Indra's net was adopted by Chinese Hua'yen Buddhists in the 7th century. This is Francis H. Cook's exposition:

"Far away in the heavenly abode of the great god Indra, there is a wonderful net which has been hung by some cunning artificer in such a manner that it stretches out indefinitely in all directions. In accordance with the extravagant tastes of deities, the artificer has hung a single glittering jewel at the net's every node, and since the net itself is infinite in dimension, the jewels are infinite in number. There hang the jewels, glittering like stars of the first magnitude, a wonderful sight to behold.

If we now arbitrarily select one of these jewels for inspection and look closely at it, we will discover that in its polished surface there are reflected all the other jewels in the net, infinite in number. Not only that, but each of the jewels reflected in this one jewel is also reflecting all the other jewels, so that the process of reflection is infinite. The Hua'yen school has been fond of this image, mentioned many times in its literature, because it symbolizes a cosmos in which there is an infinitely repeated interrelationship among all the members of the cosmos. This relationship is said to be one

---

[6] Tulsi Ram, *Atharva Veda: Authentic English Translation*, E.J. Lazarus & Company, 2013

of simultaneous mutual identity and mutual intercausality." — *Hua-yen Buddhism: The Jewel Net of Indra* (Penn State University Press 1977)

In Buddhist philosophy, the metaphor of Indra's net incorporates the concepts of sūnyatā (emptiness) pratītyasamutpāda (dependent origination) and interpenetration. Sūnyatā (emptiness) has many meanings, depending on the context and the school. Buddha nature, our spiritual core, is described as fundamentally empty. Sūnyatā has also been interpreted ontologically [the metaphysical study of the nature of being] as identifying all reality as a void, out of which every phenomenon arises and falls back into. Dependent origination is the Buddhist idea that all phenomena that arise in our perceptual field are reflections of our state of mind. This leads to interpenetration, the view that all beings, states and perceptions exist in what Cook describes as "simultaneous mutual identity and mutual intercausality".

Contemporary interpretations of Indra's net note its likeness to the hologram, a 3-D image projected by a laser. David Bohm and Karl Pribram proposed that the universe itself may be a hologram created, in part, by the human mind. Their idea was developed by Michael Talbot in *The Holographic Universe* (1992).

Indra's net has also been interpreted as affirming contemporary non-dualist thought regarding the fundamental non-local nature of mind and consciousness. Barbara O'Brien emphasises the metaphor's interbeing implications: "Interbeing refers to a teaching that all of existence is a vast nexus of causes and conditions, constantly changing, in which everything is interconnected to everything else. Thich Nhat Hanh illustrated interbeing with a simile called Clouds in Each Paper.

"If you are a poet, you will see clearly that there is a cloud floating in this sheet of paper. Without a cloud, there will be no rain; without rain, the trees cannot grow: and without trees, we cannot make paper. The cloud is essential for the paper to exist. If the cloud is not here, the sheet of paper cannot be here either. So we can say that the cloud and the paper inter-are."

O'Brien continues: "This interbeing is sometimes called the integration of universal and particular. Each of us is a particular being, and each particular being is also the entire phenomenal universe."[7]

---

[7] Barbara O'Brien, "Indra's Jewel Net", *Learn Religions* (Jun. 25, 2024, learnreligions.com/indras-jewel-net-449827).

in *The Matapaua Conversations*, which portrays the void that connects the *observer* and the observed, the latter consisting of the physical domain as expressed through the establishment and cycling of a small number of universes. That vision remains valid and is the reference point for what follows.

This fresh delivery may be read as replacing the lost ancient Indra tradition. We say "lost" because the original visionary experiences were not recorded by the people who received them. All that exist are much later literary and artistic confabulations based on oral descriptions of their visions.

We begin with the idea of emptiness, the void, which in our terms is the ultimate unmanifest, also named the Dao. From the Dao arises an intention, named the *observer*, an impersonal intent to manifest form, which in turn provides an abode for countless species to occupy. [See the multiverse model above.] This includes the human animal and its co-associate, a parasitic spiritual identity,[8] who seeks physical experience with the aim of extending its knowledge and acquiring the information it needs for its own self-transformation.

To reiterate what the self-transformational process involves, and to answer the question that human beings have repeatedly asked down through the ages, "What is a human and how does a human come into being?". At its most fundamental level, this may be answered by identifying the following movements:
- The movement of an individual node of Dao-consciousness out of the undifferentiated unmanifest, as we described earlier.

---

[8] The term "parasitic" is deliberately chosen to encourage readers to reconceive their relationship to their body, to realise that fundamentally they are not a body, they *occupy* a body. Furthermore, in relationship to its collective treatment of the planet's biosphere, the species Homo sapiens sapiens may be viewed as an infestation currently out-breeding available sources. That humanity is parasitic is currently a topic of discussion in social media and in academia. Some go so far as to call humanity a cancer. In this text, "parasitic" is not used to denigrate Homo sapiens sapiens as a species, but to remind readers that their relationship to physical existence on this planet is temporary, and that they are exploiting the opportunity to their personal benefit. Just as a parasitic microbe, plant or animal exploits a host to its own benefit, each individual human being is using their body as a host, and humanity collectively is using Earth as a host, to their own benefit. However, where a parasite in nature does as it is genetically programmed, humanity has choice. We can sensitively treat the existence and needs of other species. Or we can parasitically exploit parts of the biosphere until they die. As is currently happening.

- The movement of that node into a co-associative relationship with a physical form that is embedded in time.
- Departure from a co-associative relationship with that physical form embedded in time.

In relation to this last movement, it is necessary to acknowledge that time outside the departure does not exist, except in the metaphor of transitioning from being separate to being again unified. "Separate" refers to being separate from its own spiritual identity, and "unified" to be being united with its own spiritual identity.

Ultimately, in the case of those who co-associate with the human species, the movements of emergence and return exist at an even higher node level. This is because each embodied individual is a fragment of a node of Dao-consciousness. After they have completed their reincarnation cycle, they process everything they have experienced, learned and now know, distil it of all repetition and redundancy, and return to unity with their family of node fragments. The reconstituted, reunited, reintegrated node is then enriched by information accumulated by many identities over the course of many lives.

We offer this three part movement as a simple answer to the question, "What is a human and how does a human come into being?" With this process broadly identified, we may begin a more detailed consideration of the process of return, that is, of the movement of consciousness out of the body and back to the spiritual domain.

We begin by making the point that for the embodied to make a "return" to the spiritual domain, they don't need to cease co-associating with their body. It is possible to do so simply by connecting their lower mind to the higher mind of their spiritual self. Repeated connection establishes it as being completely normal. It is only those who denigrate such connections who persuade themselves and others it is abnormal.

The process of connection has been referred to throughout human history. Elsewhere we have referred to it as shamanic flight. As a phenomenon, shamanic flight has been experienced by individuals embodied in the human animal for at least a hundred thousand years.[9] We acknowledge that was be-

---

[9] This is when the size of the human brain was increased to facilitate more complex life experiences. This point was first made in *The Matapaua Conversations*.

fore human records were kept, so cannot be corroborated. Nevertheless, we assert it is true. In fact, the existence of consciousness within the human animal is much older than has yet been recognised. We propose a twenty-fold extension, in the order of two million years. Clearly, there is no evidence to substantiate this claim. Nonetheless, we make it.

With that clarified, we continue with our exposition, which consists of a number of corollaries extracted from the metaphor of Indra's net.

Corollary 1: Establishing a fresh perspective

Humanity's foundational myths, which followed individuals' first enquiries into their nature and existence, are unreachable due to having been poorly recorded, using only memory and the earliest systems of writing.

Our intention here is to start again, providing new ideas relevant to contemporary culture by projecting them into the lower mind of this individual. The result will be of no greater or lesser value than anything similarly shared at any time through human history. What follows simply results from another individual placing on record what he has understood after connecting with his higher self. A self that, we note, has often, erroneously, been called God.

Except in this instance, our amanuensis is not merely connected to his higher self, but to a separate, reunited, reintegrated identity comprising knowledge accumulated by experiencing somewhere in the order of a million lives. The reader may or may not grant this statement any significance. It is of no material consequence either way. Yet our perspective enables us to make a number of pragmatic observations concerning the human milieu and its trials and tribulations through history.

We could similarly discuss other species' milieus, but with less authority, because we have in our experiential set only a few other species' perspectives. Our amanuensis includes just two species in his experiential set, cetacean and, latterly, human. However, this is sufficient to appreciate, even if only theoretically, that other experiential sets may incorporate multiple species' perspectives.

We make this point to indicate that the description we are offering here is based on a very broad concept of existence. To make the most of what we are communicating, we ask our readers to accept our expanded perspective.

Indra's net is an off-world perspective. In fact, it is so far off-world it is outside the physical realm. It is also outside the realms of individual universes in the multiverse. As such, this is a privileged perspective. An unusual perspective. A seldom accessed perspective. It accommodates all humanity's concerns. But not to soothe or otherwise subdue them. Rather, it is to place them in the most expansive contextual framework available.

Corollary 2: Unlinking historical interpretations

Our first step is to state that we conceptually link the metaphor of Indra's net to the emergence of physical existence out of the ultimate unmanifest.

Accordingly, we reject the historical interpretations accumulated over the centuries. All traditional attributions to the god Indra's nature, to Indra's intention towards and influence on the physical world, all allusions to weapons and steeds, be they elephants or horses or anything else, and all theories regarding the pantheon of gods and their influence on humanity, are to be discarded. They are the inventions of prolific writers.

Historically, and recently, writers have used Indra's net as a metaphor as they attempted to make sense of natural events, such as shifting weather patterns, seasonal fluxes, floods and droughts, and other similar physical phenomena. Repeatedly, humanity has ascribed the mysterious, shifting patterns of their living conditions to one god or another.

We explicitly unlink our description from those historical interpretations. They are false, as modern science has established. With historical interpretations discarded, we return to our fresh perspective, that the metaphor of Indra's net may most usefully be considered in relation to existence on the most remote unmanifest level.

Corollary 3: Nullifying a historical injunction

As we are discussing historical errors, we reference another mistaken idea. The Christian injunction "go forth and multiply" is ultimately unproductive, because it is irrelevant to existence on the expanded scale we are describing.

The Christian injunction was intended to be implemented within a very narrow time frame. It has no validity beyond that time frame. It was only valid for a specific historical period, at the very beginning of the establishment of a politico-religious population. Those to whom it was spoken had been provided with a fresh spiritual perspective, but they were in a minority. The injunction was conceived as a means to broaden the perspective's influence in the local region.

All this means the injunction is no longer valid. In fact, transporting the injunction beyond the embryonic Christian region and across the entire Christian world has resulted in its effect multiplying out of all bounds.

Here we summarily annul that injunction!

We do so for the very good reason that the circumstances which led to it being given no longer exist. Even worse, the application of this injunction is bringing the planet to its metaphorical knees. Its influence on unbounded human multiplication currently comprises a risk to other species' survival. That cannot go unremarked. Especially from our level.

Annulment of that now invalid injunction means a Christian mother-to-be can ignore it as a factor in deciding whether or not to breed. Or breed more. If we had the power, we would erase the injunction from the Bible and from all extant derived literature.

Corollary 4: The wider impact of this annulment

As cultures mature and accumulate wealth, the demographic naturally transitions from high fertility to low fertility. Much has already been written concerning the destructive impact humanity's population growth is having on other species. Increasing infertility among portions of the human population, and the inability to properly feed other portions, sends an unmistakable and overdue message that human fecundity should be constrained. The means are at hand. Use them!

Once a balance between the human species and the planet's other species is re-established, the human population as an overweight(ed)[10] factor in modifying the climate will decline. Of course, the climate is subject to multiple and, by now, mostly well-mapped influences, the Anthropocene being just one.

---

[10] This is an ironic reference to the pandemic of obesity.

This period of history is best viewed as an opportunity for consolidation, aimed at producing well-educated, literate, numerate, computationally privileged, philosophically aware individuals. Individuals who are not confined to the narrow viewpoints promulgated by singular world views or historically encumbered religions, but individuals who are able to accommodate their perspectives to multiple viewpoints, finding commonality between them, and settling into peaceful coexistence with all species.

We envisage that if humanity can achieve that over a thousand year time frame the world's occupants will achieve a new balance.

Corollary 5: Adopting a planetary perspective

The ravages of time, which manifest in changes to geology and morphology, are ongoing. Over the millennia humanity has adapted to them. Present contrary factors notwithstanding, there is a high probability that humanity will successfully accommodate to current climate trends. This is because they now have the means to communicate across all levels of all populations. This should be sufficient for the requisite steps to be implemented without excessive resistance. That is, provided an adequate overview can be projected on the world scale.

Current resistance, particularly barriers created by personal, corporate and national interests, may cast doubt that a successful accommodation may be achieved. However, the view of the planet from space, of an interconnected but finite and fragile world, and the imagery derived from that perspective, should, if backed by sufficient campaign financing, be sufficient to influence the outlook of the world population.

We offer this positive projection as a best outcome. Of course, it may not be achieved, for the usual reasons of fragmentation and narrow-mindedness. But if sufficient support is given to organisations promoting a global perspective, and if rational discourse prevails, even using all available emotional arguments where necessary, we see a period of constructive peace-building resulting in an intercontinental balance between cultures.

It will not be easy, because invitations to contrary positions remain. Yet we maintain it is possible.

Corollary 6: Adopting a multi-life perspective

These contests between perspectives offer individuals endless opportunities to explore human experience. And to do so beyond a single-life framework.

This individual, through whom this dialogue is being delivered, has been led to expect an agrarian future in Kazakhstan. Whether that will occur in peaceful conditions is no more or less certain than the future prospects of any other individual. The rise and fall of empires provides rich opportunities for everyone to forge their own path through particular situations, or to decline to do so. Both choices provide experiences that will enhance individuals' understanding.

We mention this because the differences in scale between the individual identity and the ultimate unmanifest are vast, yet the outcomes are essentially the same. The *observer* uses the observed, that is, the physical multiverse, to extract information in the form of all the experiences, knowledge and wisdom accumulated by the vast numbers of individual beings who occupy them over vast stretches of time. Similarly, individual identities extract information from the experiences, knowledge and wisdom they accumulate over the course of incarnating over tens of thousands of years, or longer. Concern that every identity successfully utilise the opportunities available to them is the same.

Corollary 7: Indra's net updated

This brings us back to our earlier statements regarding the *observer* and the observed, and their relation to the historically conceived Indra's net.

We ask the reader to review the graphic of the multiverse provided earlier. We remind you we propose this illustration be considered an update to the historical metaphor of Indra's net.

It means there now exists a contemporary description in the English language of a vision partially recorded in Sanskrit many centuries ago. We say "partially recorded" because that, in fact, is the case. There are depths to any discussion of the relationship between the unmanifest and the physical multiverse that remain unexplored, and cannot be explored, in any language.

Given aspects of the relationship simply cannot be explained to the human mind, no discussion in any language will ever suffice. Nonetheless, we offer this thinly sketched outline to indicate the scope of what is involved, and the implications that result.

Corollary 8: Dependent origination and dying

To conclude this model of existence, we will discuss aspects of what is involved when a human body dies and the spiritual identity co-associating with it withdraws and returns to the spiritual domain.

We begin by linking this process to contemporary descriptions. The phenomenon of the near-death experience, when an identity partially retreats from its body, is well documented. This phenomenon can be confidently attributed to an individual's awareness transitioning from being enclosed by the body, its brain, and its aura's field of influence. Describing this using the terminology we prefer, a near death experience occurs when a fragment of a node of Dao-consciousness separates from the body with which it is currently co-associating, leaving it comatose.

What is interrupted in this case is the normal sharing of felt experience, which occurs between mind constructed at the local, bodily level and mind originating at the spirit sphere level.[11] As this hasn't been explained here, we will attempt to do so now.

There is no doubt that perception occurs within the human animal's brain when it merges the body's various sensory fields, combining them to construct, moment by moment, a representation of external physical appearances and reality. Experienced meditators know this.

Meditators also know it is possible to reach a point in which simultaneous sense impressions fall out of sync with each other. This leads to the meditator's awareness no longer being bound to its local physical identity, or being immersed in the stream of everyday sense data. The meditator thus realises that their everyday sense of body, identity and location are a construct,

---

[11] The human spirit exists in the shape of a sphere. This spirit sphere has a kernel at its centre that, when it chooses to co-associate with a human body, it aligns with the body's hara centre (the chakra just under the belly button). For further details see *The Kosmic Web*, Chapter 9: How a Spiritual Identity Connects with a Body, and Chapter 11: The Nature and Purpose of the Aura.

resulting from the brain processing sense data and generating responses to that data.

Alternatively, when the brain's everyday functioning is sufficiently deactivated, what comes prominently into awareness is a substratum of mind, which is itself a function of the spiritual identity. Now unconstrained by the myriad components present in sensory data streams, awareness on the spiritual level seems much clearer and much more expansive. This is because the physical body is no longer the primary locus of awareness.

Accordingly, when the brain ceases to function normally, or to function at all, awareness is no longer tethered to the body, having become detached from the senses' incessant data streams. It retreats into isolated identity and into peaceful awareness.

To make sense of this process, which has now been reported by innumerable individuals who have undergone near death experiences, you need to develop an understanding of the separate layers of identity. The five-layered model of the self, presented and discussed in detail by Keith Hill, is entirely adequate to facilitate this.[12]

That ends our theory of dependent origination. It is sufficient. We offer it to link our contemporary discussion of spiritual intent, which results in individual identities occupying a physical body, to long-standing mystical traditions within religion, spirituality and philosophy.

We now move on to consider the states of mind necessary to access these levels of understanding, and the techniques to achieve those states.

---

[12] The model of the five-layered self proposes that every embodied human identity has five layers: the biological self, the socialised self, the essence self, the energetic self and the spiritual self. The biological self incorporates the brain, limbic and cognitive systems and genetic make-up. The socialised self is shaped by family upbringing, education, culture, social norms, etc. The essence self exists at the motor, emotional and intellectual levels. It is the part of us that learns, develops skills, and forms our highest human self. The energetic self incorporates the body's electro-chemical processes, the chakras and the aura. The spiritual self is the portion of itself that the ongoing spiritual identity chooses to project into the body for that life. Generally, that varies between 20% and 80% of its full identity. For details see *Experimental Spirituality* by Keith Hill.
[12] See page 54 for the Buddhist psychological concept of dependent origination and Chapter * for a fuller discussion.

CHAPTER SIX

A New Vision

We have discussed meditation at length elsewhere. There are many meditation traditions. We have little to add regarding them, except to remark upon the efficacy of the process developed by our amanuensis. We make three points in relation to his meditation practice. The first is that memory is state-dependent.

On countering state-dependent memory

When a meditator enters a particular state of consciousness, the experience generates a set of memories. However, meditators commonly find that when they return to their everyday state of awareness they can't remember what they just experienced. This happened during last week's meditation group meeting. E., who claims to have an excellent memory, and certainly gives every indication of possessing one, was confounded when she realised she couldn't remember what she had perceived while meditating.

This leads to our second point, that it is beneficial to record a description of what one is perceiving while in an elevated meditative state. It could be argued that what we are suggesting involves a fundamental incompatibility. Meditation requires stillness of body and mind, whereas recording what is being experienced requires the meditator to actively observe and record what they observe, whether using the voice or a mechanical tool. In fact, and contrary to this difficulty, actively recording while in a meditative state is certainly possible, because our amanuensis does it regularly.

He has developed the skill of maintaining the observer role and speaking into a microphone from that role, while holding the field of awareness separate and apart from the process of making a recording. This separation minimises the possibility of the recording interfering with or contaminating the act of observing, and visa versa. The skill hinges on being able to rapidly transfer awareness from the stream of input to the stream of output and back again. The outcome is that observed phenomena, interactions and experiences are captured as they occur, making available to meditators memories that would otherwise become inaccessible once they returned to an ordinary state of awareness.

Our third point is that the efficacy of what is being recorded verbally and visually by our amanuensis is as high as has ever existed. This is made possible by advances in modern electronic technology, which guarantees a consistently excellent quality of recording. The willingness of our amanuensis to do so repeatedly, year after year, to the extent of dedicating a week or more at a time to doing very little else, besides attending to basic body care, has ensured this body of what is commonly called channelled literature supersedes, in quality, almost all other compilations in history.

An address to Peter

We come from realms to your right, which enables us to be identified as a benevolent source. Your insistence on negating and so avoiding input from the left, given its controversial character and questionable intentions, indicates you will continue to reliably make these distinctions and so refuse the standard enticements that can lead those unaware of their options into error.

Given the decades you have trained, this is to be expected. Your resilience and fortitude, which are needed to continue to make sound choices, is advantageous to us, because it indicates your ability to receive our communications in a minimally distorted manner. This has resulted in our perspectives being accurately recorded, an activity that now extends over three decades. It is our pleasure to acknowledge that and say: *Into this heart we pour love unending.*

We state this metaphorically. Our love is of the spiritual kind primarily, and simple affection secondarily. It is grounded in the utility of this connection. It suits our purposes. Those purposes remain as they have throughout these communications: to supply a refreshed series of models and metaphors regarding humanity's bi-located spiritual and physical existence, expressed in contemporary language and imagery. To that series we now add another.

More on the multiverse model

Having referred earlier to the motion of the individual on the surface of a planet performing their slow spiral track through the universe, we again shift the discussion to a larger picture, that being the image of the created multiverse as a product of the *observer* located within the ultimate unmanifest.

Inconveniently, this image doesn't allow measurements. Nor does it incorporate any comprehensible scale, either of dimension or time. This is unfortunate, because it means our statement cannot be tested empirically. It can only be taken on trust, accepted as a gift by those willing to receive it.

Nonetheless, we have included it in this text because it comprehensibly connects the personal and the universal. The multiverse image portrays a coordinating, controlling and creative relationship between an intention and its outcome. The scale of the intention is vast, as is the outcome. Both intention and outcome extend far beyond the comparatively brief instant of an individual human life. And yet, paradoxically, illustrating these matters in this way does facilitate comprehension, even if only superficially. But that is sufficient, because what we are discussing is unfathomably larger than anything the ordinary person will ever be able to perceive.

In practice, it is only to those who are able to draw on the greater capacity of their higher mind that these representations will seem probable, even natural. Assuming our readers have this capability, and that they wish to contemplate the interlinked origins of the universe, existence and life, we will now expand our previous explanations regarding their relationship to the unmanifest absolute.

Indra's net emanates from the *observer*, enmeshing the universes in a web of intention. Each universe is engendered within that web. Each universe is also bounded, and its cycles of expansion and collapse modulated, by pre-selected parameters embedded within it. Contemporary language uses the terms "big bang" and "big crunch" to colloquially reference the start and end of their expanding and contracting phases. Human speculations about these processes are limited attempts that can do no more than approximate the range and scale of what is involved.

Within scientific communities, speculation regarding whether or not any other universes exist besides the one inhabited by your own galaxy is limited to considerations of the physical manifestation of galaxies, stars and planets, and their occupation by biological life. Scientific thinkers completely avoid questions of purpose and outcome.

Contentiously, we offer the opinion that there *is* purpose behind these manifestations. That purpose is the cycling of sentience. Furthermore, when sentience is concentrated into intelligence, and when intelligent identities engage in intellectual enquiry, questions regarding the scale and purpose of their manifest universe are naturally asked.

Unfortunately, human beings have no option but to take at face value statements such as ours that describe both the nature and function of unmanifest existence, and the range of intentions possible there. Accordingly, any reader of this text has the simple choice of tentatively accepting this description, rejecting it outright, or settling somewhere between them. Our readers may allow themselves to be persuaded our statements offer a valid scenario regarding the phenomenon of their existence and life. Or they may simply ignore these discussions as too speculative and abstract, which they will inevitably and validly be seen to be, and continue to focus on their everyday life.

This last is neither an invalid nor a wrong response. There is no need for anyone to engage with these ephemeral dimensions, nor to seek to understand the purpose of their existence. Yet some do wish to engage in that kind of enquiry. It is to give some satisfaction to them that we offer these thoughts.

Deep curiosity has existed throughout the histories of all species who have sought to enquire into what exists beyond their local world. Every individual, sooner or later in their sequence of lives, seeks a comprehensive understanding of the nature of their existence and the purpose of their acquiring life, perception and love. However unsatisfactory the answers they arrive at may be. Dissatisfaction among those of any species is inevitable, due to the dimensions of space and time placing limitations on either observing or travelling beyond their local star system — except via observations by cleverly designed instruments. As a result, no biological species can ever measure the true scale of their own universe.

In this situation, all we can offer is a developmental scale of understanding, which extends from the personal, to the social, to the level that encompasses all phenomenal products of the senses, and beyond to the phenomena of experientially obtained spiritual insight. Many intelligent, questioning individuals will find this unsatisfactory, perhaps even suspect. We can do nothing about that. This is our attempt to provide a set of parameters within which these phenomena can be placed with at least a minimum of logical consistency. We offer it with love.

[Addressing Peter] We now wish to take you into the further reaches of experience, so you may capture some flavour of what we just alluded to.

Model: Species' willingness to bequest agapé

[From Peter's journal]
I have a vision of the willingness to bequest agape (WtbA) dimension within the 3-D model of agapéic space. I am looking along its axis, from minimal to maximum WtbA. I see realm upon realm, each realm demarcating an entire species, conceptually divided into volumes, each of a similar size but at integer distance. One realm is stacked behind the previous one, extending along the axis. A greenish glow outlines each division. I receive the thought that they are divided much more finely than what I am seeing and conceiving as being within a nominal unit scale of 100,000. [See graphic.]

This vision is extraordinarily extensive, but the human domain within it extends only from 48,000 to 48,000.000001.[1] Viewed from zero, the human domain is conceptually very far away, just one tiny portion of realm upon realm, effectively disappearing beyond visibility. I won't say infinity, because I don't know that.

---

[1] This tiny allocation is a reminder of the vast number of species in the universe, each occupying their nominal place on this scale.

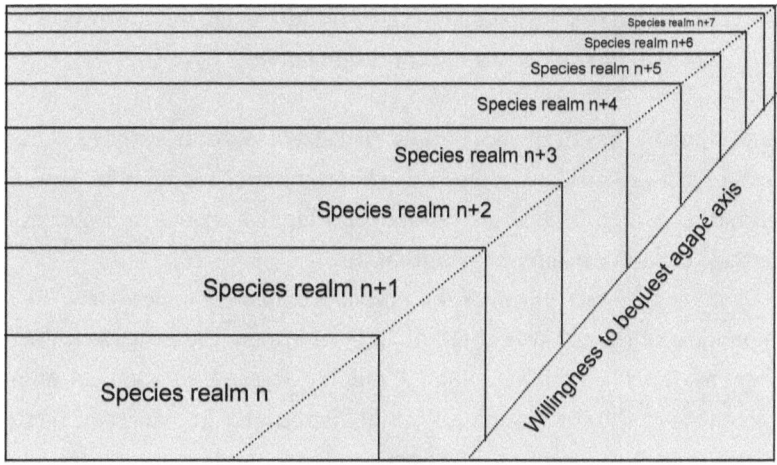

Peter's vision of species demarcated according to their willingness of bequest agapé

Vision perceived at Riverton 12 September 2018

Agapé is open, non-judgemental spiritual love. Each species has to learn to love all other beings without prejudice or judgement during the course of their incarnated existence, in whatever body they occupy and in whatever physical environment they exist. This is an incremental learning process, in which many contributing qualities, including acceptance, tolerance and self-sacrifice, are accrued life by life.

"Willingness to bequest agapé" is an attempt to capture this process in words. The WtbA scale attempts to capture the process numerically. All these numbers are notional, provided to indicate a profoundly complex process of development, the end product of which is that individuals within each species add to their identity at the spiritual level.

Within the context of their species' existence, each individual begins their incarnational cycle with low WtbA and ends with high WtbA. One point being made with this vision is that for each species low and high WtbA are different. This is not to say that one species achieves greater magnanimity than another, although to the human mind this is what the vision implies. Rather, each species is what it is. And the human species is relatively undistinguished within the full WtbA scale. Nonetheless, incarnating within the human species suits our purpose and yours, which is to become loving, knowing and wise to the extent we are able.

> It reminds me of Indra's net, which I saw yesterday on a website and didn't understand. Is this another imagined version of Indra's net? I don't know, and will have to check. At this point I can't even recall what that image was illustrating. But it may be related. Distinct lower mind confusion here!

The perspective has been successfully visualised. We acknowledge our collaborator's willingness to accept this vision without recourse to awe, nor sublimating its significance, instead appreciating that what is indicated exists on a scale beyond usual human conception.

The vision offers no more than an approximately scaled view. To accommodate all species would require a level of detail impossible to incorporate. So this is a simplified model, tailored to the limitations of human understanding. But it will suffice. Within this scale, the human range is effectively infinitesimal, even though functionally for the human multiple characteristics and possibilities are available to be explored, which offer endless learning opportunities.

This perspective may equally be applied to any zone of existence within the axis occupied by any species. For each species, willingness to bequest agapé must be navigated, negotiated and conceptually understood within the notional zone the species occupies. We ask you to remember this WtbA species scale is an imaginal model, situated in agapéic space. Both are conceptual constructs. They are simplified graphic illustrations. They are not identical with the reality of existence within actual spiritual space, in which human identities are resident.

To conclude, we are pointing to a very large picture here, essentially impossible to illustrate. Historically, it has only been glimpsed and described using allegory and metaphor. The model offered here is an attempt to provide a glimpse that is consistent with twenty-first century scientific norms. We intend to explore the implications of this perspective a little further in what follows.

CHAPTER SEVEN

—┼─┼—

Dependent Origination

We continue this conversation by addressing the ongoing vituperation directed towards the spiritual world view. Onto this metaphysical acrimony we seek to pour some calm.

More on the multiverse model

The "academic fortress" referred to in the article on Indra's net[1] is a metaphor that usefully describes the refusal to rationally analyse the history of spiritual and religious observations.

We have previously defended the validity of the shamanic world view, which was historically distributed throughout the world's cultures. Its remnants continue to have an impact in contemporary cultures. Similarly, we accept the doctrine of dependent origination, a doctrine from historical Buddhism. This is a metaphor that suitably recognises the emergence of the physical world and all biological life, which have their spiritual origins in the ultimate unmanifest. The language is suitably detached from religious zealousness, and sufficiently close to the neutral language preferred by scientists, to be suitable for our discussion here.

"Dependent origination" is, of course, an English term, translated from the original Buddhist Pali writings. An essential precondition for the term's conception was that those who formulated it had minds sufficiently open,

---

[1] *Indra's Net: Defending Hinduism's philosophical unity* (Harper Collins, 2016), by Rajiv Malhotra, obtained and consulted as a consequence of the foregoing discussion. "Academic fortress" refers to the academic rejection of spiritual experiences and metaphysical concepts.

curious, expansive and diligent to hold in their awareness the largesse of spiritual nature. By "largesse" we refer to the treasures that may be obtained as a consequence of focusing on spiritual sources, however those sources are conceived.

From our perspective, the term "dependent origination" describes the relationship between the *observer* and the observed. The *observer* we have already defined. The observed encompasses multiplexed reality: the physical realm, which emerged from the depths of the void; the physical realm's ordering into geological and biochemical patterns, which proved sufficiently stable to support the inception of environmental niches; those niches' continued existence, sufficient to make them suitable environments for species to be implanted or to migrate there; and those species having sufficient longevity that a history of their survival may be generated. Even when a species becomes extinct, due to niche conditions changing faster than the species is able to adapt, numerous other opportunities remain for the continued cycling of sentience.

Accordingly, we propose that dependent origination is a term worthy of being used outside Buddhism, as it provides terminology relevant to any twenty-first century discussion of ultimate origins.

Dependent origination relationship

By maintaining that Indra's net is a predecessor to the agapéic space model, we anchor our twenty-first century concepts in history. A wealth of knowledge has been transmitted over the millennia, especially in India. Connecting ancient and contemporary concepts allows readers to appreciate that our theoretical constructs, however odd they may appear, have historical precedents. Academics may appreciate that these ideas are therefore respectable.

The connection we are making here also offers a bridge to prior observations. The act of observation is significant, because deep ideas do not arbitrarily appear, no matter what the era. These ideas are conceived because they emerge from the deep perceptions of mystics. To describe their often novel perceptions, mystics concoct new ideas, and sometimes new terminology. Because they are describing fleeting, ephemeral perceptions, their formulations are best viewed as metaphors. Accordingly, we assert that Indra's net is a metaphor that derives from ancient mystics' ephemeral perceptions, which resulted from their deep enquiries into the nature of existence. Being a metaphor, it is best understood as pointing towards an aspect of reality, and not being a final description or definition of those aspects.

As has repeatedly occurred throughout history, after they recorded their perceptions and subsequent thoughts in writing, over the centuries others used it to generate a secondary literature. As inevitably occurs, this literature contains a mixture of valid speculations, invalid speculations and pure fantasy. As has also occurred throughout history, interventions were periodically made to address the fact that the mystics' original statements, which remain valid, had become buried under screeds of complicating and often misleading commentary. In India mystics down the centuries have taken on the task of illuminating their culture's spiritual and philosophic texts by re-perceiving what the ancient mystics perceived, then giving the original texts fresh interpretations using metaphors and terminology appropriate to the times in which they lived. We are initiating the same process here.

The virtue of this process is that it provides continuity through time, and a bridge across cultures. From era to era world views change. Anyone interpreting physical and spiritual phenomena today necessarily uses a different cultural and intellectual framework to those who lived in antiquity. As a result, in different eras no model will ever be perceived and interpreted identically. Nonetheless, the general underlying form remains recognisable, and may therefore convey impressions of the same phenomenon.

Because the unmanifest realm is inaccessible, ephemeral impressions are necessarily mystics' primary data. When they record their impressions, they necessarily use the culturally and historically determined language of their day. When that process is repeated, a series of interpretations are generated that may be traced historically through prior versions. We note that this fresh model is grounded in the original mystics' perceptions, and is not influenced by subsequent historical interpretations. Bolstering this is that our amanuensis has never read anything about Indra's net prior to yesterday and today.

To recapitulate regarding the process that occurred historically, and that is occurring here, we observe: (1) there is a phenomenon; (2) it has been observed on multiple occasions; and (3) this is merely the latest in the series. Repeated observations support the idea that the phenomenon exists. Yet observing it requires unusual circumstances, given the observer needs to be a developed mystic. This is because no one else has an interest in establishing the origins of life, nor has the patience to pursue their enquiry over an extended period of time, nor possesses a sufficiently open and subtle interpretative framework to ascribe meaning to what they perceive.

Derived from ephemeral perceptions, "dependent origination" is a concept that provides a way to describe the emergence of life from the regulating spiritual realm. "Shamanic space" is a term that points to the same phenomenon. It identifies the realm to which observers despatch their point of attention, gaining knowledge of that domain by moving within it. As a consequence, they have perceived various activities, became aware of various prescriptive forces, and encountered various inhabitants. After they returned they recorded descriptions in many languages. We seek to coordinate those descriptions. That is the reason we decided to offer this material in a general language, unmodified by concepts of the divine and its associated historical metaphors. It is a large task. We do not expect to achieve it within the lifetime of this individual. Beyond that is undetermined.

To conclude: None of these metaphors and concepts, including those of Indra's net, the *observer* and the observed, and dependent origination, should be thought of as providing "the truth". As we have stated many times now, "the truth" is inaccessible. These are no more than working concepts and models. We do not exaggerate their significance beyond that. Just as a well-trained plumber has sufficient knowledge to competently undertake the tasks involved in plumbing, so we offer these transmissions to give motivated individuals a degree of knowledge sufficient to enable them to competently navigate otherwise ephemeral domains.

Further clarification

[From Peter's journal]
Reading through the Wikipedia tract on dependent origination has made me aware of the fundamental distinction between the original Buddhist concept and what has been proposed earlier today, which links dependent origination back to the intention

of the *observer*. I wonder if further clarification is required to contextualise this statement into references, translations and interpretations across languages.

We here join the chase, as it were, to find valid interpretation. Be aware that any clarification of these topics occurs within a particular individual's mind, and that every mind is predisposed towards a different interpretation. That is, unless every mind's thinking is constrained by strict categories of meaning expressed in firmly agreed language. Given that rarely occurs, and that as a result different meanings are created moment to moment, if clarity is sought then specific distinctions in meaning have to be thoroughly mapped. Otherwise, the field of existence under consideration is so complex that everyone makes their own interpretation.

Of course, that will not do. It is a recipe for chaos. Therefore, to amplify the notion of dependent origination, we constrain discussion to the present time, using the terminology offered by this transmission, and adopting the model of agapéic space we have been developing for three decades now. The concept of dependent origination may be discussed by identifying three separate levels.

The first is on the level of the physical world being constructed via the intention of the *observer*. The physical is manifest in the form of multiple universes, the details and variations within each being dependent on the *observer's* presetting intent. Each universe's setting results in the dependent origination of environmental niches. We described this earlier. The chain of dependent origination continues, with the environmental niches being seeded with created life, which accordingly take form.

The second level occurs in relation to species as they interact with their environmental niches. All species are dependent on the occasional intervention of intelligent identities, who exercise their intent to adjust a species so it better matches changes within its environmental niche. Their purpose is to prolong the species' survival. Intervention may also involve transitioning a species from one environmental niche that limits opportunity to another that expands opportunity. Due to the impacts of randomly occurring events, physical development often occurs chaotically. Intervention by intelligent identities is in response to the dynamics involved. This occurs only very occasionally, and when a wider interest is involved.

The third level of dependent origination results from choices made by a node or node fragment of Dao-consciousness, when it elects a particular species to co-associate with for a sequence of lives. The node or node fragment uses these lives to accumulate information to educate and transform itself. The opportunities available to a species occupying an environmental niche enables an identity to progress towards a chosen outcome, and in the process to develop responsibility and understanding.

These three levels of dependent origination are fundamentally distinct. Yet each is dependent upon the other. In that sense a related Buddhist term, co-dependent arising, or co-dependent origination, is relevant.

The descriptions of these three levels are actually impossibly compressed and simplified. So much detail is involved at each level that it is sufficient to acknowledge that yes, each level exists, and that it produces outcomes reliant on pre-existing conditions. An ordinary individual doesn't need to seek more than this basic understanding. It is enough to attend to the present moment, understanding that every outcome has multiple causes. And that every outcome may be linked to multiple further outcomes. So rather than a single line of causation, a mesh of causation is the necessary consequence.

Furthermore, time does not apply to the three levels of dependent causation. Any physical individual contemplating these things is necessarily enmeshed in time, which confuses their attempts to understand how the levels interact. To resolve this conundrum, a two-level pattern of thinking is required, which involves being both inside and outside time.

Western philosophic thought, influenced by Christianity, holds that there is a causal arrow of time. Outside that context cultures depend on it less, due to a greater willingness to locate causation within a web. The Abrahamic traditions cannot easily accommodate the absence of the arrow of time, apart from those subsets who ascribe to a multiple lifetime model. And so, when attempting to provide an understanding of dependent origination, the differing reception within those two distinct cultural sets must be allowed for.

CHAPTER EIGHT

Internal and emotional self-cleansing

A disturbing dream

[From Peter's journal]
I woke this morning from a long complex dream which featured finding myself lost at some unknown distance from my home, in unfamiliar surroundings, not being able to find my way back, needing to seek help from others who were not necessarily able to assist, in a group which featured a variety of characters, some helpful and knowledgeable, some not. In particular, there was an individual who was being encouraged to pull out of himself, through his mouth, conditions of ill-health, or tendencies to that, I think. What he pulled out was a mixture, including a steel spring, various plastiky-looking things, and what even looked like dark intestines. There was no coherence, they were just random junk, one might say.

The dream disturbed me. I woke with the recognition of what this (channelling) activity is producing could, in the mind of anyone not familiar with it, be seen as wild fantasy, the product of an unhinged brain, leading to the source of the material being regarded with concern and pity, needing support for the madness he had manifested.

For a while after I woke, some 10 to 30 minutes, I was fully in the condition of recognising that perspective, and in the mental space of accepting that view as true, and that this process and its product is a manifestation of madness. It is a very long time since I have been assailed by such concerns, so it seems very odd that that has surfaced.

On the other hand, it also allows me to appreciate that perspective, if held and to whatever degree, by any other person who is not within this group-think, to use that convenient term, this bubble of belief, which might be another useful term, in which people of any religious persuasion might be seen to occupy by anybody outside of that belief-set.

So I'm a bit puzzled as to what the dream was about, its relevance, or benefit, or educational value, or whether it is just a reminder that there are entirely valid world views in which none of this makes any sense at all.

After recording the dream, I sat in meditation for one hour. I was encouraged to go very deep. I didn't quite know what that meant, but it turned out to be into unresolved issues, turmoil and grief. I eventually understood that was what I needed to attend to. Various issues arose, including the price I paid to publicly reveal the nature of P., my ex-wife.

I was being prosecuted in the magistrates' court for technical breach of a non-molestation order, imposed after I was spiritually encouraged to ring P. on her birthday, even though we were separated. "It will help you," they said. I did so, and she seized the opportunity to take me to court. When the prosecuting police sergeant asked me in some exasperation, "Why did you ring her?", I said "Because it was her birthday. I know she likes that." The atmosphere immediately changed, as all present suddenly recognised she was sufficiently vindictive to seize the opportunity of that technical breach of the court order to prosecute me, waste everybody's time and money, and cost me $500. So it succeeded in legally humiliating me, but also revealed her true nature. That resulted in instant loss of respect and reputation on her part.

That was one aspect. I recognise that the dream was a vomiting up, essentially, of unresolved issues, and what looked remarkably like intestines full of shit.

So the intention of that last meditation was clearly to explore and release, as preparation, perhaps, for something else. Or, at least, to continue the self-cleansing process on the emotional level.

With that as preamble, we will continue. The progressive cleansing of the body-mind, emotions, unresolved issues, confusions, malice, and all other destructively negative aspects resident within a person's life experience, along with influences from prior lives, is a necessary process for any individual who seeks to become a seer.

The mystic, within which we include the role of seer, is one who is necessarily cleansed of those processes and history, and is thereby able to manifest the undiminished light, and the love of its nature, in a manner supportive of all other life. And to manifest as an exemplar in their culture.

There are many lesser mystics. This author is one of them. That neither dilutes nor reduces the significance of the current dual arrangement, in which we also maintain contact with the similar lesser mystic, Keith Hill. To categorise this duo thus is not a criticism. It does them no disservice. It is simply an accurate recognition of their status in the process of bringing into the world another transmission that attempts to infuse light into a world contaminated by darkness.

It will always be the case, utopian thought notwithstanding, that the purpose of embodied life in this species on this planet is no different from embodied life in any species on any planet, across all universes, at any phase of their cycles. The purpose is to acquire love.

That being a universal truth, and there are few enough of those, it is enough to say that life on this planet is functioning as it was designed to. Therefore alarm is unnecessary. Vigilance is a different matter. As is intervention. We base this on the straightforward recognition of trends occurring on the worldwide cultural, localised social and individual levels.

The Parliament of World Religions is a suitable case in point.[1] It brings together people of good will to promote peace among all nations, cultures,

---

[1] The first Parliament was held in Chicago in 1893, in conjunction with Chicago's World Fair. Representatives from many of the world's religions attended, making it the first world interfaith meeting. Since 1993 eight more Parliaments have been held.

cults and religions, based on the principles of acknowledgement and respect, and seeking to establish stability through harmonising all with one another.

These are noble and worthy goals. We support them. However, as we expect to never participate in that organisation there is little point in carrying this message to that level. Each tradition carries the weight of too much history, as do many of those who aspire to the role of representative, which are precisely factors we seek to depart from.

"Darkness is greater than light"

[From Peter's journal]
I've sat for a short time in meditation, or at least I spent time sitting on my stool. What has come strongly to mind is the Meditation Australia Conference, held at the Australian Catholic University in Melbourne. It was my second visit to Melbourne.

Being confined to this remote country, and so not having access to the opinions of other individuals across the complex intercultural networks of religious activity and thought, I decided it was worth attending the Parliament of World Religions held in Melbourne in 2009. I was encouraged to do so during meditations at the time.

Attending the conference was useful, because it led me to further understand the variety and complexity of international belief sets embedded in religions and cultures. Attending the Parliament also updated perceptions I had obtained during my first international travel aged 21 to 23.

The experience led me to realise the futility of holding strong aspirations for having any impact on the accumulated history of any religions. Their traditions and viewpoints, so tightly held by participants in each religion, could not be expected to be impacted by any statement from someone who existed completely outside of all traditions. I therefore abandoned the attempt, understanding it to be futile.

My second visit to Melbourne, for the inaugural conference of Meditation Australia (2018), led me to the same conclusion, that attempting to share perceptions and information, was futile, given so many organisations were presenting their own perspective. And that the intention of most teachers in meditation appeared to be within either the mindfulness protocol, in which spirituality was essentially stripped from their descriptions, or their meditational activities were within a particular historically-constructed religious framework.

A university theologian who spoke on meditation and Tantra seemed to both fascinate and appall the packed auditorium with what he said. At the end of his address I was one of the few who asked a question. It was just as well I waited for the microphone, because I scarcely recognised my own voice during the interchange. It was so full of stress that I could scarcely be heard. I later realised that was because I was symbolically confronting my torturer and killer during the Inquisition, responsible for ending three of my lives.

The second thing was that, in his response — he didn't answer a significant part of my question as I recall — the theologian concluded by saying, "The darkness is greater than the light." In that moment he made plain, to my mind, that the Catholic Church has been infiltrated to very high levels, certainly within academia, or at least in the opinion or experiences of this theologian, and that the left-hand input has been very successful in capturing attention and in being sufficiently persuasive as to take the Church's path away from light, purity and sanctity. Which invalidates it as an organisation worth following or aligning with to any degree.

I think that is regrettable – but it confirms my own experience – because how else could any organisation claiming ritual sanctity have allowed such carnage to occur through history?

And so I learned that, in any tradition existing around the world now, hundreds of years can pass before any new spiritual world view gains ground. And, of course, given that the domain being discussed encompasses the timeless realm, any expectation or hope I may have of contributing to world peace through offering a broad understanding of history and spiritual identity is necessarily unrealistic.

Clearly, the objective can only be to enhance personal knowledge and let the world take care of itself.

We have a response to this situation. It has not been available previously due to the event's severe impact on you. Now is the time for it to be addressed.

Power, choice, decision

First, it is true that the Catholic Church has lost its way. That is the primary reason for its failure to maintain its position in the Western world.

Second, the Church's impact on this individual has been severe. Having lost his life at the hands of that organisation not once, not twice, but three times, legitimately casts it, in his mind, into the role of antagonist. In one sense, that is of no consequence, because it merely reinforces that the retribution the Church wreaked on him was futile. Because he returned.

On the other hand, the impact on this individual has been neither forgotten nor minimised. It has instead been incorporated into his understanding of the world, shaping where he places his allegiance, or avoids placing it. The Catholic Church is invalidated by its reactions to his choices.[2]

Third, strong forces are at work in the world, which alternatively support the survival of the Catholic Church and its decline. This equally applies to all similar organisations.

---

[2] One of Peter's incarnational choices was to become a Cathar. The Cathars lived in southern France and northern Spain and Italy during the 12th to 14th centuries. They were part of a movement that rebelled against Catholic theology and clerical control. They called themselves Good Christians. The name Cathar is from the Greek, *katharoí* (the pure ones), a term used ironically by the Inquisitors. Cathars believed human beings reincarnated until they achieve salvation. The Catholic Church judged them heretics, and murdered thousands of them. Peter has written elsewhere: "There has been another statement, which appears to have emerged from my memory: 'You'll never take me alive!' It indicates determination against opposition, a willingness to die rather than change. Also, I think, a willingness to go to the flames rather than be corrupted, either by adopting corrupt practices or corrupt beliefs, or by becoming part of a corrupt Catholic administration. I sense it is a memory of my experience of being a Cathar (~1200 CE)." Excerpted from *On Acquiring Wisdom*, p 51.

What is not widely appreciated is the extent to which individuals in every organisation claim to represent the truth and the light, but in reality undermine those aims. That this occurs is due to the fallibility of individuals working at every level. Within organisations, negative experiences stop the faint of heart from addressing issues they know are wrong, while the strong of heart are too often diverted, impeded or outright warned off as they seek to introduce light into the organisations that employ them. Meanwhile, caustic and twisted individuals, using all available means to achieve power, rise to the top, gaining direction of their own and others' organisations.

This is the nature of the human struggle. This is how those who possess sufficient personal charisma, who are able to project their opinions in either legalistic or evangelical terms, generate wider enthusiasm for goals that limit or endanger others. It is a tendency that exists in every sphere of human activity.

Only the wisest of individuals, secure in their own identity, refuse to bow down to dominant individuals and are able to use appeals to the highest principles to gather individuals of similar strong mind. Collectively, they may confront, dislodge and keep at bay individuals lusting after power.

This is the human triangle, which may be likened to the good, the bad and the ugly. Nevertheless, politics and international trade is full of it. This individual has himself encountered malevolent forces working within the oil industry.

Although we decline to characterise this competitive struggle in the language of war, it is not entirely dissimilar. However, we do not view the situation negatively, because it gives individuals the opportunity to experience the many modes of human expression. It is easy to see that those in the latter stages of their cycle of lives possess the inner resources to explore contentious roles and influential positions, and in the process may be brought into contact with individuals wielding extensive power. Whatever results from this contact becomes a useful learning experience for everyone involved.

Accordingly, it is not appropriate to publicly advocate the downfall of the Catholic Church, although some do. Nor is it appropriate to seek to undermine Christianity any more than any other religion, because every religion is so challenged. But it does show how direct, personal contact fosters an individual's appreciation of the forces at work in the world. Such forces can be denied, they can be legitimised, they can be magnified, they can be suppressed. Yet they are present, and so need to be acknowledged.

What we have for you today, then, is a meditation on the complexity of the intertwined strands of peace and discord, which are continuously present, and are therefore a valid factor in human existence. Navigating peace and discord provides choices that lead to diverse outcomes. Any individual seeking influence in the world, for which this one has only a mild aspiration, is necessarily confronted with the need to make salient choices. The challenges that follow may be gross or subtle, and may arrive disguised or needing to be eluded, but they are validly present in every moment.

Ultimately, becoming wise simply involves recognising that yes, such is the case, and that any and all varieties of choices are available within the spectrum of human awareness.

Work-life balance, 1000 year support

We have a further request. It is that the onerous task of sitting in receipt of these texts be matched by pleasurable activity. We consider it important that you have a work-life balance, so suggest a round of golf as fitting physical exercise, appropriately compensating for this activity of sitting.

We thank you for your dedication and attention so far. We wish to instil an expectation of exactly such balance in order to make this retreat destination even more reliably joyful and productive than Matapaua Bay.

Of course, nothing will happen unless there is a dedicated team willing to commit money. For that to occur, there would need to be promulgation of this endeavour more broadly than this country. In the context of the proposed foundation, or similar legal entity, to sustain this initiative in the long term — we speak in the one thousand year time frame— if that should come to pass, and if it should be supported by an international community that recognises the magnitude of this contribution, then we would be delighted to commit ongoing support to such an enterprise. And to offer continued wise steerage of that legal identity through any single or group of individuals who may elect to offer long-term support.

It is appropriate that we offer this. If our offer is not accepted for any reason, then there is no sense of loss, apart from opportunity. We would regret the lost opportunity. But alternatives can always be found over such a time period.

Golf guidance

[From Peter's journal]

Yesterday, around midday, I departed the house at Riverton and went to play a few holes of golf. I completed nine holes and noted more clearly than before an inner prompt that said things like, "Number 7 club", "Fairway driver", "Sink it!" and such-like instructions as I progressed around the course. I was curious about this, not having experienced it before.

I thought, "It sounds a bit like a spiritual assistant!" I then thought, "If that's the case, having a golf master whispering instructions in my ear, and even perhaps giving assistance in working my body in the required way to enable a more reliable performance, would really be very handy!" So I listened a little more carefully to what I heard, which was, "Act as if you have mastered the game, because in fact you already have." Well, I'm certainly not accustomed to thinking of myself as a golf pro. In fact, anything but. My progress down any given fairway is typically from the rough on one side, to the rough on the other side, and back again!

However, after relaxing sufficiently, and not attempting to use force, by the end of the nine holes I had accumulated what seemed to be a surprising improvement in my capacity to hit far and straight, in a manner otherwise not present in my progress on golf courses over the last couple of years.

This brings a new potential direction and, quite probably, an increase in enjoyment, because the tendency to self-berate would reduce quite sharply, I think, were that to be the case.

CHAPTER NINE

Life in Spirit

[From Peter's journal]
I have arrived this morning for the sixth Riverton meditation and writing retreat. At most one week's duration. I know of nothing in advance other than that it is overdue and spiritually desired. So here I am. The weather has turned cloudy, with some rain, after a lovely 2.5 days of sunny autumn. Now there are gale warnings.

Cooking dinner – curried chicken stew. I seem to have left the beef mince behind. But there is plenty of food here to sustain me. It is so long since I was on retreat I feel nervous of beginning. How strange is that!

Last night I heard, "We can see you." The difference between my living pace and retreat mode has become large. I felt driven to complete tasks ahead of winter, but haven't finished. Now my own house needs preparation prior to new tenants arriving. That is the task for the week after next. This week will allow recovery from back strain from those exertions.

Being contented

Our topic today is a purview of the features of life in spirit, in contrast to life in body. The interaction between the two being the subject of discourse in many cultures, there is merit in giving more detail concerning life in spirit, in contrast to the dynamics between that and life in body.

In accordance with our desire not to reify the information-set, nor to use traditional, culturally contaminated terminology, we will attempt a straightforward description. Contentment is a condition every person knows at some time in their life. Imagine the condition of contentment shorn of all vestiges of emotional connection and physical impacts, including of life's necessities. One arrives at a state of contentment as a condition of awareness independent of all of life's usual factors. As such, it is a mental phenomenon, not a physical or emotional phenomenon, nor a condition dependent on circumstances external to one's awareness.

Now imagine you are in a sphere. The just described condition of contentment suffuses the sphere. The sphere is neither large nor small. It is a comfortable fit. Within the sphere, your field of awareness has no particular centre, occupying the volume.

You are nowhere in particular, as defined by external references. You are simply present, not moving, unless you desire to move. Yet you remain aware, suspended in a gentle light, in an unlimited field of existence.

If desired, the field of existence may be observed as being distributed through three-dimensional space. You know others are similarly suspended within that space. But you feel no urge to be other than where you are.

You are in a condition of stasis, without duration. Time is absent, except in the most subtle of sense. Transformation does occur. But transformation occurs without reference to time. Therefore, transformation is perceived as neither slow nor fast. It is measured on developmental scales unrelated to time, being perceived instead in terms of emergence. You begin to recognise degrees of emergence, especially your own degree of emergence in relation to others. While you do not grasp after any condition other than your current condition, you recognise your condition will change.

Time is not recognised as a parameter of existence. Yet there is a process of becoming. Of coming into a condition of fullness, capacity, empathy and capability. Conditions such as jealousy, envy and comparing yourself with others are absent.

> [From Peter's journal]
> I've slept since the last transcription was completed. I was directed to read the last transcript, then heard, "Into this condition we would render you now". I'll pause the recording.
>
> I've found my meditation stool and blanket, so I'm kneel-

ing on the floor in front of the computer and table. Feeling the rhythms of my heartbeat and breathing and imaging the tranquillity that would result were even those small signals absent.

[Now in that condition ...]

No rain, no wind, no sunshine. Possibly boring?! Otherwise, content.

Becoming

What urge would drive you to leave this condition and go to some far-off hazardous place, where you are born and become muddied and stressed? Where you are challenged, sometimes so severely you are destroyed? Not once, not twice, but again and again! What urge would drive you to even be born into more than one species, all of which are foreign, unknown, challenging, hazardous? Yet that are somehow, alluringly, exciting? What impulse would drive you to do that?

What would you be seeking to become? More experienced? More knowledgeable? Possessing greater awareness? Extending your prowess into multiple fields? Would you be seeking wisdom? To become aware of the distinction between the phenomena of the body, whichever body it may be, and the phenomena of identity? To become aware of the breadth of choices available to you? To come to *know*? Instead of merely being curious, limited to wondering, to speculating, while immersed in a state of ignorance, incapable of asking questions because you don't have sufficient knowledge of the categories of your experiences? Do you have an urge to emulate the Elders?[3] But that would require comparison and desire.

Or are you driven by a need to journey and discover difference, so when you return you know the place as if for the first time? Are you driven to emerge into understanding? To become more than you have been? To expand your understanding to include categories you now have precise knowledge of, knowledge that extends into untold subtle dimensions?

Are you driven to expand your capacity to ravish, in all forms of sensual consumption, enjoyment, satiation, destruction? And, equally, to embrace the

---

[3] Elders in spirit.

most intense physical satisfactions, of conquest, tyranny, power, lust. And, having chosen and experienced them, becoming able to desist, because you now know those conditions are incompatible with the nature of love?

Thus to nurture difference, knowledge and completion? And to become incorruptible, in all its senses? With that condition being a free choice.

THAT is the reason for embodiment!

To have seen carnage and destruction at first hand, and developed distaste for it. To distance yourself from such opportunities, preferring to retire into seclusion, even sanctity. Being willing to support, but no longer destroy.

THAT is growing wiser, stronger, becoming more certain of making beneficent choices, in contrast to all other alternatives.

Being able to withstand examination and temptation, until every strand of desire for power is extinguished. To be both meek and resolute. And hence to have expanded, to have become more than you were. Filled with knowledge, having the capacity to discriminate ever more finely between choices that, on the one hand, result in good, and, on the other, support power.

Without pain in the heart due to regret. Knowing the priceless nature of such knowledge. Secure. Without need. Your capacities and empathy increased manyfold. Resolute in your willingness to care. Knowledgeable in strategies to the contrary, and declining every one, no matter which level they emerge from. Contented in knowing. Graduated from incarnation.

Peter: Jeepers!

> [From Peter's journal]
> Interestingly, the mention of pain in the heart was stimulated by experiencing exactly such pain in the centre of my chest, in or under the sternum, or in the heart chakra. I wonder if I have such regrets? And now to sleep.
> [Next day]
> I'm awake early, feeling rested and reviewing my escapade into Riverton village yesterday afternoon. I was susceptible to the idea that it was time I was better known in this little community for my activities here. A distinct feeling was associated with that desire, of urgency and desire for renown. Looking back, I see I was driven by an urge for power and influence. Comparing

that to yesterday's delivery, I find it easy to identify it as a free choice, driven not by love so much as power, so withdraw from those impulses.

I talked to a woman in the organics shop, who mentioned an ecumenical meditation group at the church with the op shop I know well. I said I was not looking for anything Christian, which led to a certain frostiness developing in her manner. The supermarket notice board was more helpful, with yoga class and massage notices. So I can pursue those if I choose, but will re-evaluate, and for the present moment merely note the urge without acting.

I also went to the Rocks for a welcome dose of calm nature. It was high tide, calm and warm here, while the West Coast is getting hammered by rain, a main road bridge being washed away. Checking the weather showed a report of the atmospheric river coming here from the tropics, having dropped >0.5m rain in places!

I'm having a little difficulty with the privation and confinement of this discipline, even though I am so well supported by love and intention on both the spiritual and physical levels. Janet said she would miss me, yet has spent so much money in renovations to make this retreat house comfortable. I am so grateful for that, and the initiative from spirit driving this whole venture.

The storm continues outside the window. The long lines of waves break, the strong offshore wind throwing spray backwards to fall on the wave behind.

I conclude from the foregoing that I remain susceptible to delusions of power and influence, hence am some distance from the state of being fully experienced to the point of satiation in the phenomena of this world. Hence unlikely to be quitting the wheel of karma anytime soon!

In a world saturated with professed works of dignified inspiration, what is the real value of more recent statements, such as this transmission? Is it just grist for the mill of publishing? A means by which more pages on social media get filled? To be viewed briefly, then passed by? Is it valid to think that someone may sometime be touched by these words and come into a better understanding of their purpose for being alive? Why else am I here? Or is all this just for my own benefit, to integrate more completely the spectrum of experience gained this time around?

Gathering informational riches

We have in mind to create a firmer foundation for you through the integration of many aspects of your life, each part of which can be articulated to the amusement, bemusement or enlightenment of others. Given your capacity for articulate language, we take as a first example the participation in drugs, as detailed in the news item just explored.[4]

Drug-taking is a universal response to life stress. Drugs imbibed across history have been constituted of every available concoction, however dangerous and however manufactured. That some die after taking drugs has been no discouragement to the desperate individual seeking alleviation from their personal demons, to use that over-used, and actually invalid, descriptor.

In cases where attached spiritual identities of some sort are actually causing difficulty, speaking generally, the drugs do little to alleviate that condition, because, of course, what is required is an exercise of competent will, either by the individual, or by another on their behalf, who is capable of wielding power and determination in the spiritual domain.

Where the so-called demons are psychological, taking action usually involves asserting a rational will in the face of the irrational impulses currently in control. That action is essential to initiating recovery from whatever is causing the ailment. In that situation, the active ingredient is neuroplasticity,[5] which is dependent on the individual's willingness to confront their wayward mind. Its "waywardness" is usually caused by an intense reaction to a terrifying event, or an extreme social or physical disturbance. Alternative inputs, in the form of therapy, promote the formation of new synaptic connections, which in turn help the wayward mind return to its prior functioning.

---

[4] This was a piece read online on cannabis usage in New Zealand.
[5] The ability of the brain to form and reorganize synaptic connections, especially in response to learning or experience or following injury.

We digress into these issues concerning the drug-based manipulation of the mind because similar transformative stimuli may be obtained by connecting to the higher-self level, or beyond. This individual has engaged in limited exploration of the mind-altering effects of drugs. Horror stories notwithstanding, doing so has informed him that by broadening one's experiences one obtains a wider interpretive net, which is useful for productively changing one's self-concept.

This retreat is an example of that process. This individual has been persuaded, on the basis of now almost-vast experience, that there is benefit in self-seclusion, in internal focus, and in being willing to look within. It is beneficial to account for the variety of thoughts and feelings, and to come to know the sub-identities within, at both the level of the subconscious local mind and the subconscious higher self, and to make both levels more accessible to the normal human consciousness. Just as neuroplasticity involves rewiring the brain's neural connections, so the explorations occurring during these retreats promote "rewiring" at the energetic and spiritual levels.

That is the type of exploration we invited yesterday, when we activated a connection to the higher mind to broadly outline a deeper understanding of the purpose of incarnation into this species, or any other — with the caveat that the species is compatible with the spiritual complexity of the consciousness in question

As usual, accessing that domain was subject to variable attention, the impact being somewhat confined to state-dependent memory. From the perspective of the local mind's ordinary awareness, the connection that was accessed, and its significance, has already come to seem minor and ephemeral. We wish to correct that perception by saying the following.

The full spectrum of an individual's bodily encounters generates an arc of development. This arc includes the local mind's development, and the integration that occurs before and after a body's dissolution, and the one after that, and the one after that, to the end of the cycle. The full spectrum of an individual's bodily encounters is a potent means to gain a "handle"[6] — a computing term only recently understood by this individual — on each aspect of experience encountered within the physical domain.

---

[6] A handle (like the handle on a broom or a screwdriver) is a convenient way to hold some more complex object. When an object is stored in a database or library, its handle

Manipulating an experiential "handle" involves wrenching it to expose the contents of the experience in question, then fitting the extracted information, including all the multiplexed cues, images, feelings, thoughts, and everything else related to the experience in question, into the scaffolding network of previously acquired knowledge. This process brings complex analysis to bear on each component of every experience. It results in the construction of a mesh

---

provides a way to refer to or draw on that object without needing to open out the object in all its complexity. In computing, a handle is an abstract reference to a resource stored elsewhere. The handle enables it to be used without the user needing to unpack it in all its complexity. Using the term handle in a psychospiritual context, it may be applied most appropriately when an individual is between lives. A handle then becomes a tool useful for analysing units of experience. Each unit of experience, such as results from playing the role of parent, or soldier, or maniac (among many), is in fact a multi-layered complex made up of sense impressions, conditioned attitudes, a propensity to act in certain ways and not others, intense emotions, wild, defensive over-reaching thoughts, pre-life plans, successes and mistakes in their execution, etc. A handle becomes a useful referent when evaluating that unit of experience alongside other units of experience, and deciding which to draw on in subsequent lives. This is a complex relation, not easy to describe. We will try.

Each life involves a number of units of experience. One easily grasped example is in relation to roles. A role may be thought of as a unit of experience. Each individual takes on a number of roles in a life. These may few or many, with each role being more or less complex. During the course of a lifetime elements within each unit of experience overlap, and perhaps interact: being a child, then raising a child, is an obvious example of the latter. Because so much is packed into each role, its associated unit of experience is extremely difficult to unpick and comprehend while in an embodied state, and especially when you are still living through them. But in a non-embodied state thought itself exists in clumps, that is, thought is not a singular stream, easily externally influenced, or a chaotic jumble, as applies when embodied. In the non-embodied state, thought is inherently multiplexed. This means that many factors are easily held in thought simultaneously, enabling the individual to make connections in a way not available to the far more limited human brain.

In this context of non-embodied thinking, a "handle" becomes a practical tool, as it identifies multiple layers of experiential knowledge. So when the role of parent or soldier is being chosen for an upcoming life, the handle for "mother" or "soldier" may be wrenched open in order to identify which factors will be drawn, to be used, to be grappled with, to be battled against, to be corrected, or developed, or perfected, in the upcoming life. In effect, a new role is chosen for the next life that becomes a sub-unit of meaning in relation to the larger unit that is the role as it has been performed previously through multiple lives. Aspects from that extended role are selected for the upcoming life. Psychospiritually, the term "handle" encompasses all this.

of connection extending across a vast network, which is available to be placed and interpreted within known or emerging parameters of understanding. The purpose of doing so is to gain secure knowledge regarding what it is to be alive, as well as to exist. The distinction is not trite.

An individual initially comes into existence as a spiritual identity by emerging from the unmanifest Dao, first in the form of a node, then, in the case of those who co-associate with the species Homo sapiens sapiens, as a node fragment. This has been discussed in full elsewhere.[7] We will not repeat it here, assuming what has previously been described. An individual subsequently co-associates with body after body, each one subtly different, each located in subtly or grossly different circumstances, culture and time period, using the resulting opportunities to harvest from their experiences information accessible while living in a body. And, generally speaking, inaccessible while not.

[Loud rain is audible in the background.]

To illustrate this, we draw attention to the rainstorm. Feeling the impact of weather, becoming wet and cold, suffering from hunger, being far from the social support encompassed by the word "home", being stressed to exhaustion — these are experiences inaccessible to an individual existing in a non-embodied state. Each individual is singularly enriched by experiencing them, integrating them into their personal network of understanding, and developing an appreciation of which related experiences may be acceptable or rejected, and to be sought in the future, or not.

Familiarity acquired through multiple lifetimes naturally leads to stress levels reducing. In a very experienced individual, everything that happens is instantly and pre-consciously accounted for, resulting in no anxiety, but rather simple understanding. And so such individuals develop an ability to experience calm rather than be shocked by the new.

In stating this, we are referring, in part, to the merit of this individual being willing to personally encounter diverse experiences, both in this lifetime and in others. Every incarnated individual willing to encounter diverse experience is enriching themselves in the same manner.

---

[7] For an introduction to this process see *Learning Who You Are* pp 17-32. More detail is provided in *The Kosmic Web* pp 33-70. Emergence from the Dao is also discussed extensively in the Michael Teachings books and related websites.

We acknowledge the objection that if one assumes the time frame of a single lifetime, a life may be short compared to the average. So the short-lived individual may be viewed as having missed out on something valuable, because all their potential experiences and the consequent learning is lost. Our perspective is that a short-term, one lifetime view is inappropriate, given some lives are naturally longer and others naturally shorter, and the individual will incarnate again. Accordingly, development needs to be appreciated as a long-term and not a short-term process.

In that sense, when an individual is consciously fearless, and risks their life and loses it, this is as much a cause to celebrate their embodied existence as another who extends their lifetime to their biological organism's maximum. So while we do not advocate high-risk entertainment for its own sake, we acknowledge each individual has an infinite variety of possibilities to explore. If not sooner, then later. Carelessness with a life is never wise. But it is not fatal.

Peter: Mmm. It obviously pays to ask questions!

CHAPTER TEN

—⊢⊢—

Metaphors of Agapéic Space

Mussel farm model

[From Peter's journal]
Helen Wambach wrote several books detailing her findings researching her subject's recall of prior lives. She used hypnosis to facilitate regressions amongst groups of people in order to give them an opportunity to explore prior lives. I obtained a copy of *Reliving Past Lives*, which seems to me to be an important reference point in the modern investigation of reincarnation, because of her sample size of 1088 participants. She computed the male-female ratio of the other-life personalities recalled by participants, and found it matched historical records of male-female birth ratio. That suggests something real was remembered, and their recall was not just fantasy.

Towards the end of the text, she briefly discusses her contemporary model of existence, including patterns of connection between people, utilising the metaphor of the apple tree, where each apple is a life lived, or the present life. Regression facilitates an excursion from ordinary waking consciousness, through the "tree's" network of branches, in order to access the content of different "apples".

A similar mussel-farm model spontaneously emerged one Sunday afternoon in Gore during the meditation group meeting. I unexpectedly found myself spontaneously describing the model. In a similar manner to the way mussels accumulate on a rope suspended in seawater, an increasing cluster of lifetime personalities associate together, each linked to the fragment of the node of Dao-consciousness, which in turn links to every other node fragment of Dao-consciousness within the complete node. Once all required lifetimes are completed, the cluster of clusters eventually amalgamates into a unity.

It is a finite model, like the apple-tree model, with the distinction being that in the apple-tree model the roots are associated with, or notionally inserted into, the ground of all being.

We take this opportunity to comment on the two related models, each an attempt to connect mundane reality to the network of individuals' lived experiences.

One uses the metaphor of fruit growing on a tree, drawing sustenance

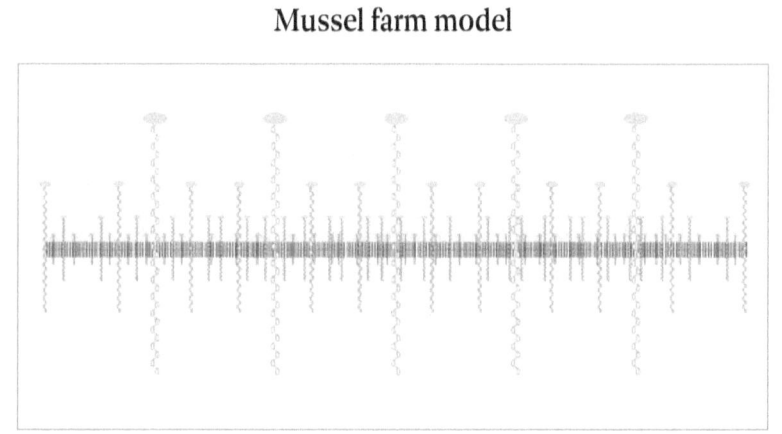

Mussel farm model

This shows in simplified form a horizontally-distributed network of communication links between node fragments of Dao-conciousness at the higher-self level. Conceptually appended to each fragment is the vertical string of as yet unintegrated personalities developed within each lifetime. Union of all fragments eventually occurs. This entire set of approximately 1000 fragments comprises one node of Dao-consciousness. There are uncountably many such nodes. Estimates of their number are futile.

from nutrients in the environment, including the sun, rain and fertile soil, to form an apple. The other is of a collection of mussels, tethered to a surface float, hanging vertically in sea water, similarly drawing nutrients from its local environment in order to grow. To offer an abstract description, apples and mussels are examples of coordinating networks that draw sustenance from one aspect of existence, accumulate it, and use the accumulation to enrich another aspect of existence.

But what these two models do not do is delve into the deeper issue of why apples and mussels exist. Certainly, both are harvested for consumption by other species, including the human. But there is a deeper purpose involved in the creation of such coordinating networks. That is the intention of Life itself – and we deliberately use the capitalised term, Life, as a metaphor that is sufficiently remote and all-encompassing to reference the intention behind this networking activity. The intention we are referring to is exploration.

We earlier commented on the Christian injunction, "go forth and multiply". In the context of this discussion, we propose rephrasing that phrase into "go forth and explore, and return bearing your acquired experience". What is acquired may be thought of as gifts, the reward for making the effort to explore. That remote flowering (remote because in the physical realm) is subsequently gathered during the process of reintegration by each node of Dao-consciousness as it journeys from emergence to return.

The ultimate unmanifest, which we denote Dao-consciousness, is the largest container, the largest accumulator, of human experience. Its richness extends far beyond what the human mind could ever conceive. This is what may genuinely be regarded as the infinite mind, exercising infinite purpose, recognisable through the cycling of cycles within cycles that exist within the cycle of spiritual emergence and return, which can never be observed, and to which no time scale is relevant.

In this context, the apple and mussel farm models are correct. But they are limited. They are just models created by human minds attempting to summarise their understanding. The models do not reflect reality, the ultimate purpose of which is inaccessible and therefore remains opaque.

Accordingly, no matter how well an individual at the level of their human personality is integrated into any given life, and no matter how successful it may be in accessing its own larger identity across multiple personalities, and no matter if it is even able to occasionally access an individual personality of another fragment of the entire node of Dao-consciousness, it remains incapable of accessing and comprehending the Whole. An individual's awareness may be likened to that of one grain of sand on one beach. With there being an incomprehensible number of other beaches, each containing an uncountable number of grains of sand. The impossibility of understanding the scope of this reality renders human attempts to understand the Whole not just impossible, but irrelevant to their existence. Which doesn't render these two models irrelevant. They have value. But it is a reminder that all human concepts are at best models which highlight a small sliver of reality.

That said, a final conclusion may be drawn. We have described emergence and return on the level of the individual identity's personality level, at the group soul level, at the super soul level, and at the level of the incomprehensible Whole.[1] In that sense, our task is complete. And, in relation to this individual's exploration of existence and the meaning of life, it can be held to be complete. And to be a success.

Any person now living is similarly capable of understanding these models, to the extent they choose to scrutinise them, and find in them a meaning for their own existence, and a means to appreciate their personal history involving travails and joys, desperation and hope.

Recognising a soulmate

The idea of a soulmate is prevalent in both Western and Eastern cultures. What is lacking is an appreciation of the depth of the interactive networks that are active during their social encounters. That an individual stands out

---

[1] More specifically, these four levels of emergence and return consist of : (1) at the single life level, of an individual node fragment projecting part of itself into a human body just before birth to form a new personality, and when that personality's body dies reabsorbing it back into itself, along with all that was experienced in co-association with the personality, a process that is repeated an average 1,000 times, until the node fragment has become so enriched, and learned so much, it no longer needs to incarnate; (2) at the node level, in which a node fragment reintegrates with all its fellow node fragments, reconstituting into a node that is vastly enriched compared to its state when it originally emerged from the Dao; (3) the node's return to the Dao; and (4) the entirety of the multiple universes that originally emerged from the Dao finally returning to it.

significantly from the crowd is recognised, but the reason is not understood. We wish to illuminate this issue.

We begin by drawing attention to the field of agapéic space, within which connections pre-exist, but which do so below the threshold of normal awareness. When two individuals come into physical proximity, those pre-existing connections generate an inner excitation sufficiently strong to rise above the threshold of attention, and makes it unambiguously clear to one, or both, that they know one another. If that leads to the development of a social relationship, it is in fact merely amplifying their pre-existing spiritual level connection.

A common difficulty is that when those involved lack awareness of the cause of their connection, yet they nonetheless seek to explain why they feel so significantly linked, many misattributions result. We wish to anchor into public awareness that the significance arises from their being linked on the spiritual level, a linkage that pre-exists their conception. Life plans and karma are key factors that determine whether individuals who know one another from previous times, in other places, will associate with one another during a particular life.

This offers a simple explanation for feelings of recognition, of being drawn to the person on the basis of that recognition, or of experiencing ambivalence towards that person, to the extent of feeling repelled by them, or alternatively having a feeling of being instantly safe, which occurs in rare cases when a loved one is recognised.

Spiritual formation: awareness of models

[From Peter's journal]
Using internet search tools, I have attempted to find cultural references to the idea of direction in spiritual space relative to the body. I can only find references in which physical direction is combined with spiritual direction, along with attributions concerning astrological-style collocations of quality, meaning, direction and time. Australian Aboriginal dreamtime sets of meanings, as discussed by Mircea Eliade, have some slight relevance. It seems to me improbable that the model of agapéic space in this

transmission[2] should be original. However, it might be the case that any such set of ideas is subsequently mixed with concepts related only to the physical world and the human world.

The situation is simple. The realisation that there is a dichotomy between physical existence and spiritual existence has led to the generation of maps regarding humanity's origin in spiritual existence. Just as humanity has invented maps to navigate through the physical world, so it has also created metaphysical maps to navigate through spiritual realms. Both sets of maps have been adopted, then adjusted, as more details become known regarding existence in each realm.

What we offer is novel. It has not existed prior to this century. It will eventually come to be recognised as having both relevance and truth value, if only within the limitations of its application. The caveat is that the utility of what we are offering will be confined to those individuals who seek to orient themselves in relation to their deeper identity. It is completely irrelevant to those not wishing to do so. What we offer has explanatory power only for individuals interested in delving into the subtle phenomena they experience, who cast about for appropriate descriptions and interpretations, and who seek relevant maps that help them do so.

The idea of spiritual formation is relevant to this discussion, in the traditional sense of building a beautiful soul, to use that language. For this to occur, what is required is that an individual becomes aware of their spiritual life existing alongside their physical life, and that they wish to transcend the limitations of their embodied human nature and seek to align more closely to their spiritual nature. This transformation, in which the manifest lower mind emphasises and adheres to the qualities and values inherent to spiritual nature, has been adopted through most of history by sensitive individuals who find value and virtue in those practices.

In this sense, they aspire to liken themselves to the highest cultural ideal of their time. This is the case where cultural ideals are modelled on truth, beauty and goodness, ideals that support spiritual formation. Other cultural ideals, which model the virtues of power, aggression, combat, plunder and

---

[2] Referring to the ideas initially recorded in *The Matapaua Conversations*.

territorial control, are less useful for spiritual formation. In fact, they actively counter it.

The approach promoted by this transmission and its models explicitly supports spiritual formation as a product of meditative practice. Practice naturally leads to communication with the higher self. We are providing accurate explanations regarding the spiritual phenomena encountered through that practise. If these explanations are maintained without being tainted by reference to physical experiences and related explanations and maps, and if those who seek to promote their own spiritual formation sustain their efforts, then clarity will continue regarding the distinction between spiritual life and incarnated life, with all its attendant emotions, confusions, and concerns about relationship and survival.

Countering fears that human consciousness does not survive bodily death, this spiritual world view supports inevitable survival through a succession of bodies.

CHAPTER ELEVEN

—┼─┼—

Protocols for Meditation

[From Peter's journal]
I've asked the question as to why, yesterday morning, I experienced a complete reversal of my attachment to, and living life within, the spiritual world view. I spent between 10 and 30 minutes fully immersed in the non-spiritual, perhaps atheistic, world view, where everything I ordinarily occupy is believed to be fantasy and nonsense (because viewed as no more than pure conjecture), of zero applicability to any sane person. I wonder why that event occurred. But I think now it's a cogent reminder that few people occupy this space to the degree I do.

The purpose of the intervention into your usual mindset was to remind you that viewpoints in the world are diverse and are held with equal if not greater tenacity than yours concerning what is right, true and proper. These viewpoints are validly adopted by many people, even though the specialised perspective occupied by an individual such as yourself is incomprehensible to them.

Your willingness to respond supportively to our agenda is a cause for ongoing celebration. The reticence you feel regarding our agenda is a simple product of the rebuffs, incarcerations and killings you experienced at other times. So we understand completely the resulting limited capacity to act. Nevertheless, more bold action will soon be required. We seek to prepare you for that.

The extension of meditation group activity to the adjacent city of Invercargill offers a means to slightly extend your personal reach, along with our influence, to those few who would seek to benefit from it. Do not expect it to be large, yet neither will it be zero.

Meditation group protocols

Group meditation will be conducted according to the following principles.

It is open access, not a private group.

In the spirit of service, it will meet at such a place and time suited to the most potential participants.

Participants are not members, except in the most general sense.

Participants are primarily meditators in training.

Training is to be conducted in an identical fashion to the Gore group, and the Hamilton group before that.

It is expected that meditators will act not as chelas, disciples, subordinates or anything other than equals, because that is what they are.

Acquiring the skill of enhanced perceptivity through the process of meditating is no different from acquiring any other skill. The only distinction is in the degree to which individuals accept and access their own spiritual sense-set, conventionally termed the opening of the heart and third eye.

We explicitly include the crown chakra, which embodies understanding and acceptance of incarnation into multiple bodies, and which enhances the process by adding to the information acquired at the higher self level.

None of this should be contentious in the slightest. Every individual attracted to the group will already understand these things, with very few exceptions. It will be easy, fun, and occasionally profound.

Lingering spirits and elementals

The spiritual clearing of lingering spirits in the lower South Island is currently only partially attended to. Lingering spirits are often found around cemeteries, because after people die their bodies are placed there. Unsure where to go next, the spirit lingers. Those whose body is cremated tend to linger around places familiar to them before death. Alternatively, those spirits who know where to go next have no difficulty doing so.

The issue of land clearance is complemented by the presence of other significant spiritual identities. These are elementals, who have chosen to be responsible for various geographic features of land and water, rivers and streams, mountains and clouds.

The presence of elementals of cloud and, by implication, of weather, is not well known. Nevertheless, a population of elementals occupy the airy reaches of the sky. It is possible, on occasion, to interact with them.

The elementals of land and water are much better known, although scarcely recognised locally, let alone to the extent that their location is plotted on a map. We would prefer that were done. Partly, this is to revive the tradition of respectfully acknowledging the love expressed via their attention. It is also to publicly acknowledge their existence in an open manner.

The current focus on materialism, on consumption, on entertainment that is generally created far away, means that opportunities to go where elementals are across the landscape, and to openly acknowledge them and enjoy interaction with them, has become a vanishingly small enterprise. We would resurrect it. Because ignoring that population of identities, whose task they have taken on out of love for the myriad creatures that populate the landscape, locks unaware individuals into only a small fraction of life. We would change that.

Part of the issue is that historically elementals have been viewed as strange, or even malevolent. With extremely rare exceptions, that is not the case. Occasionally an individual subconsciously wishes for education, and begins to interact with such an identity, drawing benefit from the relationship. This is commonly regarded as special, and especially spooky, itself a product of fear. We propose countering historical attitudes grounded in fear by openly acknowledging the existence and nature of elementals. To aid this process, we suggest the following.

We propose the group itself be the place where invitations to interact with elementals be circulated. That is much more appropriate than advertising in the public domain. In due course, through word of mouth, the invitation will reach those interested, who may then be initiated into the experience.

It is expected that every experience of interaction will be recorded in all its details, including time, date and GPS coordinates, and that these records will be stored in a database. This way, each replication will consolidate the probability that this is not a mere personal imagining, but a replicable event involving the actual presence of an elemental.

With these standards for reporting and recording in place, a map can begin to be constructed. We are not being frivolous in requesting GPS coordinates. Every smartphone, when loaded with the appropriate software, has the capacity to access GPS. Given the software's free availability, any intelligent person is able to make the appropriate observations and place them on record.

Doing so necessarily requires access to a map scaled better than 1:50,000. 1:20,000 is scarcely acceptable. The actual placing of marks on a map held in software is the second step. Knowledge of the distinctions and conversions between GPS coordinates and map grid designations is required. National land data organisations have such tools.

CHAPTER TWELVE

—┼┼—

The Triple Screen Model

We have further material to transfer during the last days of this retreat. From this point, the constant checking of news is to cease. Nothing else of national or international significance is expected to take place in these few days. Your retirement into a condition more resembling the strict Vipassana mode is required to enable the transfer of more, and more obscure, material. As has been the case in the past, we wish to facilitate not only your learning, but also generate a text to facilitate others' understanding of the process of living and dying on this planet. We now take your awareness into another realm.

> [From Peter's journal]
> I'm seeing in my field of view a full screen-width of a curious mixture of green and orange colour, uniformly distributed, with the orange forming a fine distributed dot-like or pixilated network. I'll close the roller blinds fully in order to take the sunlight out of the equation.
>
> I've unequivocally established that what I'm observing is the product of my physical eyes, because when I place my hands in front of the field of view, it changes and becomes darker. So at this point I have no sound basis for perceiving the other realm I was told I would be directed to. [The illustrated model appears.]

The triple screen model

The triple screen model draws on the information screens of different sizes found everywhere today. Presenting this model is an attempt to use a familiar metaphor to describe an easily understood procedure, which uses protocols adopted by meditators throughout history to access spiritual level information.

Entering the arena beyond the body, which we call shamanic space, is a simple matter of shifting the focus of awareness through to the third screen of our triple-screen model. Yet while simple in theory, doing so requires some practice.

Physical and social isolation is usually required as a pre-condition to facilitate the easy transition of awareness back and forth. Sitting in quiet, the mind then needs to be emptied. This may be likened to a video screen's fade to blank effect, when an onscreen image dissolves into blackness. The blackness then becomes a transparent field, which in this model we are designating the imaginal layer. Deeper layers of perception may then be projected onto the transparent blackness.

A shift in the focus of attention between the physical and imaginal layers is routine when reading. Written descriptions stimulate the memory, which projects imagery into the mind. This imagery is separate from the words being read. The extensive arrays of imagery collected over the last century by mechanical and electronic means has created an extensive library of landscapes and objects, which vastly extends the available imagery to the human

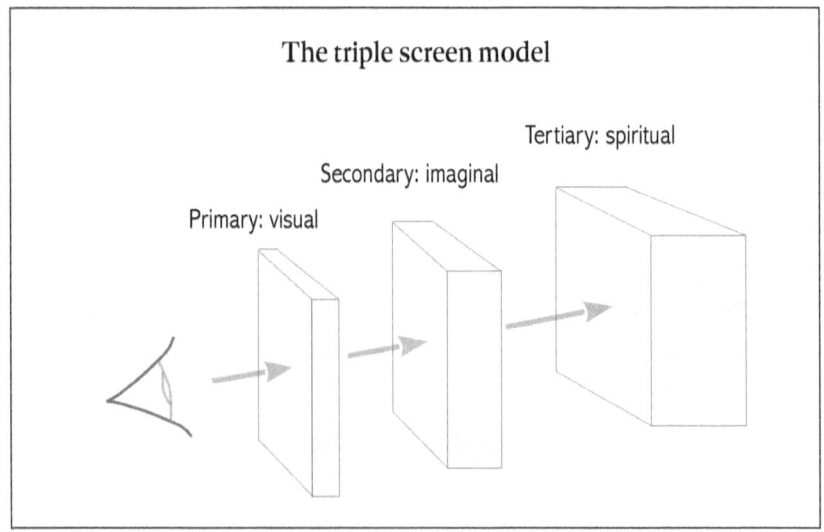

mind beyond direct personal experience, which is largely all meditators in previous centuries had to draw on.

The process thus involves two simultaneous streams. One stream is sense data, the other consists of visualisations and emotional states projected at the imaginal level. In the case of reading or watching a screen, each stream is continuous, with the person's attention shifting easily and naturally between what they are seeing and their imaginal response to what is seen. While we are discussing visual sense data here, the same process applies to the other bodily senses of hearing, smell, taste and touch. Each involves two data streams, consisting of the sensory input and the imaginal level response. While the percipient is usually engrossed in the sensory input and the remembered images, smells, sounds, tastes and touches triggered by that data, what is actually occurring is the process of meaning construction.

The construction of meaning simply involves making sense of arriving data. The process entails drawing on previously acquired information and attitudes, including what has been learned through education, assumptions and beliefs inculcated via familial and social conditioning, and stances and sentiments shaped by prior experiences. This complex pool of consciously and unconsciously amassed material provides the data that the mind draws on when generating an imaginal level response to a sensory input. That process usually occurs unconsciously.

What is not acknowledged in contemporary descriptions of meaning construction is that the pool of material an individual accesses may also contain sense data acquired during other lifetimes. It is only occasionally drawn on. But that it is occurring becomes apparent when an individual experiences an imaginal level response that has unusual depth and resonance.

We have just noted that drawing on other-life experiences is intermittent. But it may also be continuous. A small subset of individuals are able to access memory sequences outside the space-time of their current life. This is accessible as a result of deep enquiry. If such memories were not worked for but surface in this life, then the deep enquiry occurred in previous lives. If an individual has no framework to process the memory and give it context, then the memory will resonate deeply, but will remain puzzling. This provides one explanation for the deja-vu experience, although it is not the only one.

That the construction of meaning involves making sense of incoming sense data by drawing on prior conditioning, learning and memory is well known. We now wish to take the discussion beyond the contemporary model and consider spiritual input.

The extent to which any person is willing to imagine the possibility of being able to perceive beyond the first screen level of sense data, and beyond momentary meaning-making and the momentary construction of content projected at the level of the imaginal screen, depends on them being willing to accept that they are a spiritual being, accept spiritual space exists, and accept the multi-life model we are advocating here. These three are requirements for anyone who wishes to consciously project their attention beyond the first two screens and into shamanic space. If they have not been indoctrinated to fear what is to be found there, or if they have been so indoctrinated but have reprogrammed themselves sufficiently to rise above fear-projected fantasies, then natural human inquisitiveness will project their attention into that domain and discover identities to interact with there.

We need to emphasise the role the imaginal level plays in the process of spiritual level exploration. The incarnated human awareness, even when it enters the spiritual beyond, remains embodied. It remains conditioned by a lifetime of sense-grounded experiences, which are reinforced by social conditioning. So when spiritual input impacts their awareness, it is inevitably interpreted first in terms of everyday physical phenomenon, then using inculcated ideas.

To offer an example of the first. When Peter is reached out to from our level, he experiences it as a physical chill. In fact, his aura is being pressed, but his body-centred cognitive system interprets that energetic input as physical sensory input. An example of the second is when people interpret the presence of a spiritual identity as an angel or devil. This is an example of religious conditioning interfering with perception. The problem is that thinking one is perceiving an angel fosters feelings of awe and submissiveness, along with feelings of being special, while the devil fosters fear and an automatic response of running away. Both sets of responses prevent the individual from receiving what is being communicated. We note that perceptions that a spiritual identity intends harm, and so has a devilish intent, are almost entirely due to the individual being so frightened that they project their own fear onto the identity, which intends no harm. This is why religious conditioning becomes a hinderance to those who wish to explore their own spiritual possibilities.

The point we are making is that significant work needs to be done at the imaginal level, undoing socially inculcated false concepts and doctrines, and addressing one's own psychological shortcomings, before spiritual input can be received open-mindedly, without prejudice and bias.

To complete this digression from the three screen model, there are occasions when an individual's awareness rise completely beyond the limitations of their bodily and imaginal inputs. This involves what may be termed a full blown mystical experience, experienced by an individual just once or twice in a lifetime as a reminder of what their innate nature consists of.

In this century, a more common occasion in which individuals' awareness lifts beyond their limiting bodily and imaginal inputs occurs during a near death experience, during which they perceive with a clarity not available to them in their ordinary embodied awareness. However, it is instructive that when they return to their body, and attempt to make sense of their experience, some individuals reference heaven and hell and angels and devils. Religious conditioning dominates their meaning making. This is not a negative outcome, given they may have to continue to live in a religious community, so using socially accepted terminology is a way for their experiences to be accepted. Nonetheless, those who undergo mystic experiences need to be aware of the extent to which pre-conditioning, religious and scientific, shapes and often skews perfectly valid spiritual perceptions.

The principal virtue of the triple screen model is that it provides a non-religious context for contextualising the variety of natural perceptions, their levels, and the varying frequency of perceptions on each. Sense data flows continuously. Meaning-making is generally continuous. Combining sense data and imaginal concepts to create meaning essentially occurs continuously. For most people, the exception is accessing shamanic space. Only a small subset of human individuals are capable of directing their attention into shamanic space at will, and so receive information from that domain with any frequency.

Full spectrum living is predicated on being able to appreciate that there are levels of sensing, which are accompanied by their associated flows of information. In order to access the different levels, it is beneficial to have a theoretical understanding of what is occurring. That is why we offer this three screen model. We are clarifying that the embodied human being has three primary levels of attention.

For those who seek to expand their awareness to incorporate spiritual knowledge and experience, being aware of the level at which their attention is operating is of primary significance. The focus of one's attention is usually an unconscious response to input. During the course of a day attention is automatically captured by a succession of inputs: waking, abluting, dressing, responding to family, breakfasting, hearing the news, and so on. In order to become an alert, intelligent participant in the spiritual dimension of one's life, it is necessary to learn to intentionally disengage one's attention from the mundane realm and direct it into non-mundane domains. One's awareness then becomes open to non-sensory input.

A key question that facilitates this process is, "Where has the information just received come from?" It is helpful to have an open-minded attitude regarding shamanic space and the phenomena that occurs within it. Projecting feelings that the experience is special, and that the percipient is special because of that, are not helpful. It is more helpful to have a casual attitude and simple, straightforward responses.

Historically, over-hyped responses have contaminated religious traditions, giving spiritual encounters undue significance, giving them the status of the divine, and elevating them beyond the human everyday. We consider it is more useful to appreciate that data from shamanic space is of no greater significance than sensory and imaginal data.

That is the basis for our insistence, shared now over a period of several decades, that balanced weighting be assigned to information arriving from all the three domains under discussion here. All love is special, no matter in what realm it is experienced, and so is every other input experienced by incarnated human beings. An unbalanced response is unnecessary.

Perceiving a reintegrated node

[From Peter's journal, adding to the previous entry]
The triple-screen model does not preclude interference from

more than one input channel. So this example may include multiple overlaid perceptions, with the shadow cast by my own hand across the field of view observable, but not irrevocably defining the case.

[Next morning]

I've slept enough. The song *Killer Queen* (by Queen, 1974) is strongly present in my mind. The weather has calmed.

[During the next meditation session Peter was given another vision, this time of an enormous spherical form, very bright, of which he could see just a small portion. The sphere was the spiritual form of those who are collectively the source of this transmission. The encounter illustrates many of the points made in the preceding section.]

The size relationship between you and us may be likened to that between the Sun and this planet. This is not literally the case, being only indicative of our comparative relationship. Several implications may be derived from this vision.

What you are perceiving results from being the object of attention from our level. You are not currently the sole focus of our attention, nor do we continuously sustain our attention in this manner. What you perceive is a product of the moment.

Your perception of our relative sizes is responsible for embodied recipients historically attributing awe to the object of their perception. This is not necessary. There is no difference in intrinsic value between us.

Human awareness is dominated by the body in which it resides. Social conditioning regarding comparative magnitude, particularly that the physical is lesser compared to what historically has been termed the divine, generates a bias that skews an appreciation of intrinsic value and leads to the human-involved aspect of identity being convinced of its inferior status.

This social conditioning is a form of confirmation bias: the human mind is conditioned to assume the human is lesser, so when a spiritual level perception occurs that preconditioning automatically leads the individual to consider itself inferior. Later, after the perception has passed, the mind thinks its perception has confirmed its assumption, and therefore the perceptual evidence confirms that it really is inferior. Actually, the precept has shaped the perception. That is, the recipient enters the perception assuming it is inferior, so during the perception it projects the notion that it is inferior. In fact, nothing could be further from the truth.

This present personality is unwilling to attribute either a radically lesser value to itself, or to manufacture awe in relation to what is perceived. This is appropriate. Such an attitude lays the foundations of a new tradition, in which equal value is ascribed to perceiver and perceived, no matter the relative status of embodiment nor differences in accumulated experience.

Traditionally, humans have given a radically different value to reunited reintegrated nodes of Dao-consciousness such as us, inevitably attributing us god-like status. Consequently, they are so shocked during an encounter with those entities like us, their mind is so overwhelmed, that they lose consciousness and fall to the ground. That this is not the case here is a sure indicator of emotional maturity, of well-generated and anchored beliefs concerning essential equality, and of sufficient processing of conscious and unconscious fear to allow it.

Your perception of increased heat within your body is a simple consequence of proximity and of the energy flow from us towards you. That "warmth in our gaze" that you feel, and which you are construing as being similar to the social interaction of parent and child, is another example of the way social conditioning biases perceptions during spiritual interactions. There is no warmth in the gaze, just simple recognition as allies in our shared endeavour. In this particular instance, the endeavour is to support the formation of a reconstituted, rebalanced description of the relationship possible between allies like us in spirit.

Of course, there is unlimited positive regard. There are manifestations of interaction, as we have just described. There are plans to be discussed. There are conditions to be sustained. There is goodwill, flowing in both directions, to be recognised. There is appreciation of the difference in accumulated experience, but without submissiveness in either direction. Rather, there is an honouring of the sustained effort to foster accumulated development.

In that context, then, it is possible to say the following: First, the plan is proceeding well. Second, it is unfinished. Third, its duration exceeds the lifetime of this biological organism. Fourth, we have others we are fostering and communicating with in this same manner.

In time, and as these transmissions accumulate, a small set of human individuals will be recognised as having performed this same role. Comparing transcripts will enable a refreshed description of fundamental purpose for incarnation to be assembled interculturally. This will facilitate an increased understanding of the reason the human world has such a variety of experiences, and how that variety benefits human beings.

Right now, none of that matters. We offer it only for the sake of uninvolved individuals who come across this transmission and wish to evaluate it. Naturally, such evaluators will have to work to form an unbiased view.

Individuals who engage with our intention and who are willing to be exposed to the related privations are inevitably few. That does not make them special. They have merely acquired particular understanding. Every professional, in whatever field, acquires a specialised breadth and depth of understanding. All deserve recognition and to be valued for doing so. This individual is no different, except recognition and valuing will only come long after this formation of personality and bodily organism have ceased to physically exist. Which is of no importance, because the role persists much longer than that.

> [From Peter's journal]
> At this point, the connection telescoped back into invisibility, the sense of presence extinguished, and I was back fully and only in the present, my awareness confined to present space-time in body.
>
> Phew! Well, damn me, that was interesting! I perceived an enormous spherical form, of which I could see only maybe 10% of the surface. I had the sense it was extremely bright, but there appeared to be a grey neutral filter, there for my protection, given our difference in energy levels. That perception of warmth, the "warmth of the gaze", has gone now. It was REALLY nice! With that kind of maternal caring quality perhaps encapsulated in the phrase, "You dear little thing, you!"
>
> That was out of the blue. I had no idea it was coming. And

here I am, here again! Invigorated! It provides something like an automatic reinvigoration of purpose, and a recommitment to the role and task, with no room for doubt.

The previous reference to having the song *Killer Queen* going through my head (before this meditation session began) could vaguely be considered a precognition, because that node of Dao-consciousness (NDC) could so easily be considered a queen and so easily be viewed as slaying false perception. Or some such. I feel a bit excited and a bit like dancing for joy :-) That's really unusual for me!

(Note: The connotations of bi-sexuality and androgyny apply equally to the notion of queenly status relevant here. There was no sexuality present at all, of course. I've used those references humorously as complex cultural analogues of feeling.)

[That evening]

Having met the originator of these transmissions again, what am I to make of it? The contrast between the Theosophical view encapsulated in the phrase "the dewdrop slips into the shining sea" comes to mind as an example of possibly invalid universalising of the reintegration process mentioned at the end of *The Matapaua Conversations*.[1] If that is true for a node of Dao-consciousness, that comprises in the human case a set of ~1 x 10E3 fragments, each accumulating ~1 x 10E3 personality formations. So it is the particular case of each personality formation that "slips into the shining NDC" during its process of integration after graduation from embodiment.

That accounts only for ~1 x 10E6 humans existing throughout history. The multiple millions of humans living through the multiple centuries of human existence requires many more than just one NDC. So although the process for human spiritual identities may be universal, the final destinations must be multiple and into finite sets as defined by each NDC's initial fragmenting.

---

[1] See pages 186 to 190, where the criteria for completing our cycle of incarnating on this planet, and the process for reintegrating with other node fragments, are described.

The mentors comment: "This adequately defines the process and outcome."

Therefore if each NDC may be experienced as containing god-like nature in comparison to the inexperienced human personality who encounters one, then there are many "gods". That each is not truly of that nature is beside the point, that is in terms of explaining the history of such encounters during shamanic flight, reverie and dreams.

Choosing appropriate language

As you are refreshed by food and drink, we can now continue. Our objective today is to continue the elicitation and elucidation of first-hand experience, and its interpretation, in order to provide a refreshed set of descriptions regarding the nature and scale of human experience within the zone of manifestation known colloquially as the spiritual domain. We identify it differently, in unfamiliar terminology.

That domain contains many levels, with the terminology appropriate to describe each level differing somewhat, one level to another. Of course, the highest levels cannot be described in English, as there are no descriptive terms suitable for explaining such rarefied levels. And even the term "rarefied" carries connotations inappropriate to the situation.

The more modest levels, of relevance to an identity encapsulated in human form, are more frequently encountered, therefore some terminology is more familiar. We note these terms include glow, fly, levitate, and diminish and expand. Related emotions occasionally felt include exultation, fear, harmony, disquiet, tumult, smoothness.

These are all terms relevant to conditions experienced while in ordinary consciousness, or in an only slightly altered state, through which one accesses the auric envelope or the spiritual sphere that encapsulates it. Shining, dullness, texture and opaqueness are descriptions that may be attributed to the external appearance of the spirit sphere, while flow and colour are terms that may be attributed to auric perceptions.

These terminologies, along with their analogues and equivalents, abound in both historical and contemporary descriptions of conditions experienced by any person successfully encountering those levels of perception. They further include darkness, gloom, points of light, shadows, shades [an archaic term for disembodied spirits], impressions of eyes looking, impressions of one's own eyes seeing, or of a single eye seeing with monocular vision that is incapable of resolving distance. These are attributes of seeking, and being in receipt of, visual perceptions, or interpretations of being intentionally observed by others located in the spiritual domain.

It may be seen there is an extensive history of language used to describe activity, travel and encounters, once an individual has taken their point of perception outside of the confines of their body.

Among different individuals, this complexity of interaction inevitably produces both direct, clear and accurate perceptions, and mistaken interpretations and confusion. Therefore selecting terminology to describe these classes of perception and experience is a fraught exercise. Exact description is almost impossible, given the extent to which observations are coloured by prior experience, and by expectations that prevail within the culture in which one has been raised. Hence any investigator has a multiplicity of terms they need to negotiate with and navigate through before they can select their own sets of metaphors and technical terms.

We have attempted to provide unifying principles in order to avoid terminologies that have too much disparity. We have also, in almost all cases, confined our terms to one language, in this case English. In addition, we have attempted to confine our terminology to contemporary metaphors, with a preference for technical metaphor, and a bias towards mathematical description, where that has utility. In fact, its utility is small, with the application of computing metaphors being of extremely limited use. Alternatively, the language of number offers some opportunities to describe situations simply and with exactitude.

Despite all this, we consider it necessary to primarily use language that is welcoming, and that facilitates a broad reach, because the domain under discussion is effectively infinite, and it contains diverse phenomena. Hence to ensure as much as possible that our language is relatable, we have used metaphors drawn from the familiar human physical and social world. Outside that, we occasionally use arcane terminology, because nothing else is available.

CHAPTER TWELVE

—┼┼—

Violence, Love, Wisdom

We come on the final day of this short retreat series to, first, offer accolades that sufficient attention has been directed towards us that some of what we wish to say has been captured. That there is always more to say is merely a consequence of our intention to project another spiritual transmission into the physical domain on this planet.

We say "on this planet" because, of course, there are many other planets, many other embodied species, and many other civilisations, some of which are also always in need of refreshed metaphors and perspectives to counter the errors their traditions have accumulated. It is not necessarily that those traditions are incorrect, merely that they have been corrupted by speculation through time, due to insufficient care given to maintaining a distinction between each tradition's foundational understanding, provided via the original specifying descriptions, and the elaborating speculations built on them. This process occurs universally. The human case is not exceptional.

To sum up, a broad perspective of existence is required to accommodate a spiritual perspective. That it has taken our amanuensis half a lifetime to come to a balanced appreciation of the distinctions between the modes of experience in body, outside the body, and while disembodied, indicates the radical challenge of achieving this.

In the human population as a whole, it is a rare achievement, of zero relevance to most of the population. That this possibility is nonetheless of interest to a certain percentage reflects the degree to which they have recall and feel that their embodied lives are better for being aware of where they came from.

It is unfortunate when such recall and feeling is translated into a series of rules, and that breaking them be considered a justification for killing. That is not wise. Nor is it the intention of any spiritual identity. When an injunction to kill is used by an ambitious few who seek power over others, whether in their flock or in the wider population, it is a sure indicator that what is at play is not intended from the spiritual domain, but is wholly an act of political will and confined to the human domain.

We state that in relation to events that recently occurred in this small country in the South Pacific,[1] which we have followed and acknowledge. We offer a few comments on what happened. Our comments are not for those who are suffering because those they love have been deprived of life. They are rather for the curious few who seek a broader perspective on such events.

Political violence

The event itself was intended to be a lesson inflicted on the Muslim community in that city. The roots of the impulse to kill were generated within the perpetrator by events inflicted on him, and at times on her, by males of that culture. The antagonism runs deep, and across centuries, in the same way that this individual [Peter] has been motivated all his life to live beyond the clutches of Christianity. Due to the negative impact of Islamic beliefs on the perpetrator, he came to view the religion as abhorrent. So he has derived particular satisfaction from his actions. He is unbending, and will remain so during this lifetime, refusing to bow down and be accountable for his actions. That is the depth of his hatred. He is not alone.

We use this instance to point out that there is a continuing impact on individuals who have lost their lives at other times, in other places, at great cost and in terrible pain. Such occasions impress on them what they view as the unfair distinctions regarding who is acceptable and unacceptable, which are made within the community that rejected and punished them. When undying spiritual love is perverted into an excuse to inflict terminal injury, that perversion itself should more appropriately be condemned.

And yet, because history is full of such injustice, and individual after

---

[1] Muslims praying in a mosque were murdered in 2019, in Christchurch, New Zealand.

individual, and sometimes groups, even multitudes, have been subjected to slaughter, in greater or lesser pain, and of greater or lesser duration, those events become formulae that echo through generation after generation of individuals, who, as they come back into the human world, continue to be reminded of, and to feel the impact of, such terrible mistreatment.

What is required is empathy, understanding and forgiveness. The individual especially needs an opportunity to self-interrogate, using widely available techniques of introspection, self-inquiry, and catalytic emotional expression, so they may express their pain and come to peace within the current lifetime. When that is the case, rather than the usual summary justice being meted out, what becomes possible is a divergence from a trend that will otherwise extend across lifetimes, decreasing the likelihood the individuals involved will inflict their pain on others again.

Supportive analytic treatment has the potential to change the direction of individuals whose capacity to love has been distorted. It will reduce their tendency to be born into future populations still carrying their burdens of pain and guilt, and their desire to inflict pain on others in the same way it was inflicted on them. We urge recognition that such possibilities exist. We urge such strategies be adopted in relation to those incarcerated due to their destructive behaviour.

The most potent techniques need to be applied. Of course, not in a coercive manner. Only when the individual comes to understand that they will benefit from willingly adopting the strategies of self-cleansing in relation to their accumulated pain can the proven techniques of spiritual intervention, chemical intervention, and psychological intervention, be tenderly applied to assist their transformation.

Coercion must have no place. This perpetrator's malign behaviour is a product of past pain. Seeing such individuals as damaged before birth relieves them of the worst accountability for their actions. Transformation, at their choice, is the only valid treatment the custodial authorities may make if they wish to be supportive. Such perpetrators may be resistant, and go to the end of their life unrepentant. Nonetheless, after their physical embodiment is over they will regret their actions and seek their own betterment by reducing their karma in subsequent lifetimes.

There is no need for custodial authorities to terminate perpetrators' lives, as doing so ignores that perpetrators' attitudes have been shaped across multiple lifetimes. While killing a perpetrator may seem like the quick cheap fix, it just reinforces unprocessed alienation.

The excuse of ignorance is no longer tenable among custodial authorities. Remediation through psychological transformation and spiritual reconnection is the only supportive way to enable perpetrators to, in their own time, transform themselves. These skills are readily available in most, but not all populations, internationally. That they are not currently in vogue is a consequence of ignorance and historically constructed unloving, even vindictive, attitudes. These are collective cultural pains, disconnected from humanity's needs when a broad view is adopted.

Peter: Well, I think that's helpful. But I'm sceptical of that perspective holding sway in this culture in my lifetime!

Accumulating wisdom and love

[Peter's journal]
Reflecting this morning on Indra's net after re-reading the foregoing, I finally understood that it comprises both the intention of the observer to construct the physical domain, via the multiverse, and the spiritual domain out of the unmanifest absolute.

So the *observer* is Indra, as identified by its primary products and means of creating them. To which the mentors stated, "Oh ancient *observer*, deified no more!"

I also understand that the phrase, "We come on this final day of this short retreat series ...", means that this day's entry is the final chapter of the book. It can now be edited by me, the graphics prepared, and presented to Keith for publication.

With the working title of *Southern Nights and the Light of Awareness*, a first draft may indeed now be assembled from the material collected to date at Riverton. Conceptualisation of the resulting product can be left as usual to the colleague Keith Hill and his fertile connection.

We conclude by reiterating that the reason for entering the physical human domain is that it provides the opportunity to learn, through direct experience, what otherwise remains only a theoretical or speculative enquiry. The ethical dilemmas that inevitably occur during the course even of a normal and quiet human life are unavailable to an individual existing only in the spiritual realm. Incarnation creates an enormous advantage, in the sense that the opportunity to directly observe, and play a role in, the turmoil that results when working through a succession of ethical dilemmas demands a high degree of mental and emotional focus, which leads to the accumulation of wisdom. Acquiring focus and wisdom is significant because they are both a function of, and facilitate the further growth of, a loving nature. Which is what one engages in incarnation to develop.

Time is essentially absent from the spiritual realm. So it doesn't matter whether development occurs slowly or quickly. This means attempts to accelerate the process have no meaning. In this time-bound realm, generating a story that an accelerated path out of this veil of tears exists, and should be preferred, creates a compelling argument. However, it has no basis in fact. The acquisition of a balanced perspective occurs irrespective of demanding deadlines. On that basis, the inevitable dilemmas, rule making and rule breaking, and the multivarious pressures of a human life, can be embraced with fortitude and patience, finding enjoyment at every turn.

Epilogue

Early this morning the thought came to you that you, and therefore our input, is far "down the food chain" in terms of this country's social and academic communities. Yet we suggest this has equally provided an opportunity to articulate what we intend to convey into this culture and time. In that sense, there has been full freedom. There has been zero necessity to limit our articulations to conventional metaphors, conventional ideas, historical dogma and, especially, protected established doctrine. Instead, we have total freedom. This is an unusual situation.

That starting point, from a condition in which all doctrinal elements are rejected, is uncommon, in the sense that most published mystics, and most ordinary spiritual people, are already indoctrinated into specific cultural and spiritual world views. Accordingly, when spiritual ideas are projected towards them, out of respect for both their situation and their beliefs, what is conveyed to them is biased towards their preferred forms. Wishing such recipients no harm, whatever is imparted to them is necessarily couched in phrases that they understand and accept, that is, using ideas that are not too anomalous in relation to their doctrinal position.

The freedom here, in this ongoing exchange, has been that from the beginning we have had to deal with little doctrine. This is because you have been inculcated with very little indoctrination. If there was any indoctrination at all, it was a dislike of being conditioned into any established religious framework or set of beliefs. Such conditioning as you have had has supported freedom of articulation. That conditioning, primarily resulting from a secular education, provided both academic freedom and discipline, backed by the values of goodness, forbearance, truthfulness and general honesty. This has resulted in you being in a sound position to accurately record the statements received. That has been productive to date, resulting in a well-documented delivery containing a number of perennial themes, augmented by some that are novel.

It is our opinion, therefore, that given sufficient time for discovery and incorporation into the academic mainstream, this outlier of spiritual records will eventually be examined and accorded some validity. That it has yet to receive that treatment is of no consequence whatsoever, because the time frame allowed for its recognition is at least a century.

We have no qualms about its contemporary appeal to others, or its rejection by them. In due time that will change. Those currently interested will persist; those currently aware of it and rejecting it, for whatever reason, will soon pass into history. Providing plans for its archiving are carried out, this record will persist.

So we come on this occasion to recognise and acknowledge this fleeting moment of the inception into a new decade and a new year, and find there continuing opportunity to say the things that we wish to be placed on record. This is not the last of what we intend to say.

APPENDIX

Nodes of Dao-Consciousness

The Dao is the ultimate unmanifest. Everything that exists derives from the Dao. Within the Dao we have identified the *observer* as the initiator of the experiment that is the multiverse.

It needs to be understood that the *observer* is not a personal manifestation of any kind. It cannot be associated with God. What we have attempted to express through the term *observer* is best thought of as an intent within the Dao. That intent, as we observed, is filled with goodwill, intelligence and love, plus many other qualities that cannot be expressed in human language because there is no equivalent experience in the human domain.

For example, the Dao in its intent is magnanimous and expansive in a way that human existence, focused on the much narrower concerns of the physical self, is incapable of manifesting. Even when the human spiritual identity is in a non-embodied state, which is actually its natural state, it would be overwhelmed if it was exposed to the expansive magnanimity of the Dao—and the term "expansive magnanimity" is a meagre attempt to capture the fullness of what the Dao is. Again we can only fail to make the inexplicable explicable. But the gesture is made.

So when thinking of the *observer*, think of an abstract intent that cannot be fully described. It is an urge. A momentum. That is all. Certainly, do not conjure in your mind the image of a being of any kind.

We began this chapter by asserting that everything that exists comes from the Dao, from the ultimate unmanifest. This includes all spiritual identities, which we are here naming nodes of Dao-consciousness. This is because, along with intent, consciousness is intrinsic to the Dao and derives from it.

Nodes are cast from the Dao

The Dao's nature is to manifest nodes. Nodes are individual agglomerations of consciousness that are cast from the Dao—by "cast from the Dao" we refer to the spontaneous natural development of a node that consists of the same substance as the Dao. Of course, the term *substance* is false, for the nature of the Dao has no substance in a conventional sense. So a node of Dao-consciousness may be thought of as a spontaneously agglomerated product of Dao-nature.

The arising of a node of Dao-consciousness is a spontaneous event triggered by a local accretion in density. A suitable metaphor is that of the ocean undergoing turbulent conditions, and as a result spontaneously emitting droplets from wave tips. This is a perfectly adequate metaphor, given that chaotic conditions in the sea generate forces sufficient to fragment the water, just as forces within the Dao generate something like tidal pressures. As a result, a variety of droplets come into being.

Nodes of Dao-consciousness are these droplets. Like droplets, nodes consist of various magnitudes and complexity. We will discuss the significance of nodal magnitude and complexity presently. But first we need to discuss what happens to a node when it first becomes manifest.

The state of the inexperienced node

When first cast from the Dao the node has little self-awareness. It can be barely differentiated from the unmanifest from which it is freshly accreted. Given it is of the same nature, it feels associated with the unmanifest, to the extent that it sees little difference between itself and the tidal forces which led to its manifestation. It is still bobbing on the wave, so to speak, by which it was cast from the Dao. Development is required for it to begin to identify itself as distinct from the infinite unmanifest.

Gradually, the node becomes aware of its situation. It perceives others of like nature around it. It becomes motivated to find out more about where it is and who it is with. It learns from those who are like it that various dimensions of existence are available for exploration. It also learns that it is possible for it to eventually make its way back to the ultimate unmanifest from which it was cast. There is an underlay of excitement in learning this. It discovers it can explore. And it becomes eager to do so.

As the node manifests its intent to explore, others respond. So it finds community. Within that community is information. But the information is not easily understood by the node. The node doesn't know enough, and it lacks the inner resources to comprehend what it instinctively knows is available and may be understood. It becomes aware of this because it can see that many of those it is with possess extensive knowledge, love and wisdom. It feels frustrated. So now, having developed a strong sense of its own limitations, and being motivated to extend itself beyond those limitations, it seeks opportunities to learn and grow.

Accordingly, it enquires regarding the specific opportunities available to it so it may become loving and wise like others in its new-found community. It discovers appropriate opportunities have been mapped and thoroughly understood by those who possess greater experience. The community offers advice and counselling. This increases the node's awareness of what options may be preferred for self-development, which the opportunities are now seen as offering. By this means it is educated regarding what opportunities are most appropriate, and given the information it needs to make its first forays into learning.

Individuals at this stage are dew-drops, to use traditional terminology, conscious atoms, to use alternative terminology, novice spirits, to use a term from Spiritualism. They may otherwise be identified as inexperienced nodes of Dao-consciousness seeking their first association with a physical species.

How a node matures

When a node of Dao-consciousness co-associates with a physical species it inevitably starts to learn certain things. It becomes aware of its place within the order of life. This includes developing a sense of its relationship to other levels within populations of nodes. And it acquires information, knowledge and understanding, as a result of which its opportunities for taking on responsibility are enhanced.

It is through such experience that a node matures. And as it matures it becomes suited to explore more complex opportunities that are commensurate with its increased maturity.

A familiar model from the human world indicates this maturing process. An individual working in a large organisation can progressively ascend through the organisation, from the bottom to the top. As it does so, it acquires information relevant to each level. As it rises, it takes on more and more responsibility in relation to others, especially those directly under its care.

This exact same process applies to maturing nodes of Dao-consciousness. Although there is a proviso. At the human social level, as equally at the spiritual level, there are ranges and spheres of responsibility. According to the capacities a node possesses as a consequence of being cast from the Dao, so there are corresponding levels of responsibility to which it may aspire and eventually achieve.

Hence the specific qualities of each node's Dao-nature is reflected in what it aspires to in any environment, what kinds of information it seeks out and by hard work acquires, and how it processes that information to develop a mature understanding.

One other issue needs to be discussed at this point in relation to nodes. That is the issue of fragmentation.

The fragmenting and re-uniting of nodes

Not all nodes remain whole and complete throughout their existence. Some nodes spontaneously fragment after their emergence from the Dao. They do so for the same purpose that drives all nodes: to facilitate exploration and enhance their learning process.

Different nodes fragment into different numbers of fragments. There is a basic correlation between the size of the node and the number of its fragments. Larger nodes fragment into more nodes, smaller nodes into fewer. This is true as a general statement, but there are exceptions. There is no need for us to describe the exceptions as they are not relevant to human experience.

Fragmentation that *is* relevant to human experience includes those nodes that co-associate with the human, as well as with the horse and the cetacean family, consisting of whales, dolphins and porpoises. These nodes do fragment. In the case of human beings and cetaceans, it is the individual fragments that occupy bodies, sequentially, one body at a time.

As regards numbers of fragments, nodes that co-associate with the human species fracture, on average, into one thousand individual fragments. This number is approximate. Some human-related nodes fracture into fewer fragments, some into more. Nodes that co-associate with horses and cetaceans fracture into fewer fragments than the human. We will deal with these nodes and their related species elsewhere, as it falls outside the purview of this text.

Do all fragments of a node select to incarnate in the one species? Generally, yes. This is in part because they all receive the same advice from those who possess the same quality of Dao-nature. It is also because they wish to engage in their cycle of incarnations with those they know, these principally being other fragments of the same node, or fragments of other nodes closely associated with their own.

Nonetheless, some fragments do choose to co-associate with more than one species. And some select to co-associate with species on other planets completely, whether in this or in other galaxies. They may even explore opportunities offered by a species existing in a different universe. Selection is made entirely on the grounds that what is chosen offers useful and appropriate experiences. Given each fragment has choice, all this is possible. And so, inevitably, some choose to do so. That includes some who also choose to occupy human bodies.

Each node of Dao-consciousness possesses all the qualities of the Dao. These qualities include identity, intellect and purpose. Consequently, each individual fragment of a node also possesses identity, intellect and purpose. So you who are reading this transmission are a fragment of a node of Dao-consciousness. You have individual identity, intellect and purpose. You have self-creativity and choice. You have utilised these qualities to shape all your prior incarnations for the purpose of experiencing and learning. And you will continue to utilise them to evolve according to your self-creative intent.

Fragmentation leads to another phenomenon that applies only to nodes that fragment. This is that at the end of their maturation cycles all of a node's fragments come back together to reunite and form what was earlier called the group soul. In the context of what we are now discussing, it can be said that the group soul is a reintegrated node of Dao-consciousness.

After all a node's fragments have matured sufficiently, they are designated as having completed their cycles of reincarnation. They then reunite with every other fragment from the same node. In doing so, each one brings back everything they have experienced and learned, every skill they have developed, the wisdom generated from every responsibility they have taken on and successfully negotiated. As a result, the node is incalculably enriched in comparison to its initial inexperienced state.

Underlying each exploration is the drive for enrichment. Enrichment of the individual. Enrichment of whatever environment a fragment occupies to which it can contribute. Enrichment of the node when the stage of reunification is reached. And enrichment at other levels beyond that of the reunified node, levels we will not discuss here. The process of enrichment goes all the way back to the Dao, to which everything is eventually returned.

The image of a node emerging from the Dao, spontaneously fragmenting, and its thousand or so fragments then independently spreading out through the kosmos to explore, experience, interact, learn and evolve, could sound to some like a process a writer of science fiction might concoct. Nonetheless, it is true.

The physical multiverse is your domain. The expansive dimensions of spiritual space are your domain. Embodied realms, non-embodied realms—they all present opportunities for inquisitive nodes and their questing fragments. You are currently bound to a physical form. And you have definitely made a commitment to co-associate for a time with the human species in order to work through the conditions and experiments you yourself have set in train. But this will not always be so. When you take your place within a reunified node of Dao-consciousness, the kosmos in all its variety and vastness will await your engagement. The experiment is that vast and that fascinating. And it is as exciting as you choose to make it.

— This is an excerpt from *The Kosmic Web*, pp 42-47.

Glossary

Agapé: From the Greek, meaning selfless love. The word was subsequently adopted by Christian theologians to describe non-physical, spiritual love. Agapé is the nature intrinsic to Dao-consciousness.

Agapé frequency: One of three fundamental axes that define agapéic space. It has a scale comprising a nominal range of 1 – 100,000 discrete realms.

Agapéic space: A model and metaphor generated to describe spiritual existence. Agapéic space is defined by three axes at right angles to one another, these being agapéic frequency, hierarchy and willingness to bequeath agapé. Agapéic space comprises the totality of existence, including the physical, astral and clear light domains.

Amanuensis: A literary assistant who takes dictation or copies manuscripts. Here, a person who receives information from non-embodied entities.

Ask (of spirit): Spiritual identities commonly only communicate with human beings as a result of being asked. This enables them to avoid revoking any individual human being's free will.

Aura: The formative structure in the implicate order which partially defines the human physical body.

Auric channel: Refers to the aura's capacity to channel information from the spiritual domain to an incarnate individual's ordinary lower mind.

Awareness: A state of elementary or undifferentiated consciousness.

Bio-identity: Identity at the physical human level, constituting a body, a biologically associated mind, and a personality. The bio-identity's mind is also called the lower mind. Co-associates with a Dao-identity.

Coalesence, co-association, co-habit: The process by which an individual spiritual identity unites with, and animates, a human body.

Channel: A human being who serves as the medium for transmission, facilitating the movement of information between spiritual and physical domains.

Clear light: Spiritual space perceived beyond the dim astral level. Experiences of this domain have been placed on the historical record by mystics.

Consciousness: Consciousness comes from, and is a node of, Dao. It functions on two levels, Dao-consciousness and bio-consciousness.

Dantian: Historically, the Chinese term (*tan tien*) refers to an energy centre in the body located in the belly, approximately two finger widths below the navel. The Japanese term *hara* (meaning belly) is equivalent and commonly used interchangeably. The *tan tien* has been described as being "like the root of the tree of life". These terms refer to a different and deeper level of identity and function than the Indian term chakra, which relates to the aura. Within this text dantian is used to designate the kernel of the spirit-sphere when it is coalesced with its chosen body. *See Identity (spiritual)*.

Dao (Tao): The ultimate source of all that exists. The ultimate unmanifest.

Dao-identity: Identity at the spiritual level. In the case of the human, this is constituted of a fragment of a node of Dao-consciousness. It contains the qualities of the Dao, including intellect, purpose and self-creativity. Co-associates with a bio-identity.

Dependent origination: A historical Buddhist concept, adapted here into a metaphor suitable for discussing the emergence of the physical world and biological life, which spiritually originate from the ultimate unmanifest.

Divinity: A religious term, now out-moded, because it erroneously promotes the separation of the physical and the spiritual, and creates a hierarchical relationship between those who are embodied and those who are not.

Emergence: On the cosmic level, emergence is a feature of the expansionary cycle of each universe. On the biological level, emergence is a process whereby life as a whole develops from lesser to greater complexity. Biologically, this also applies to species. On the spiritual level, emergence is a process whereby nodes manifest from the Dao.

Empirical: Based on, concerned with, or verified by using sense-based observation or experience, as opposed to theory or pure logic.

Energy (particle): An electrophysical phenomenon measured in electron volts.

Energy (physical): The capacity to do work.

Energy signature (spiritual): A complex array of information encoded within the aura that conveys all of an identity's characteristics. Perception of an energy signature enables the perceiver to assess another's character and trustworthiness, and hence to evaluate the risk of interacting.

Group soul: A node of Dao-consciousness. Among those nodes that fragment in order to explore and mature, when they complete their cycles of incarnation they reunite and form a unified group soul.

Hara: Japanese for belly. It is an energy centre located approximately two finger-widths below the navel. As such, it is a patterning on the electrospiritual level derived from the implicate order. It is also the level on which the spirit-sphere manifests, and so may be interpreted as the level of actual human spiritual existence.

Hierarchy (social): A system or organization in which people are ranked above or below one another according to status or authority.

Hierarchy (spiritual): The attribute which constitutes the sum and product of loving acts throughout a life as one builds on one's history in other lifetimes.

Higher mind: A function of the higher self that processes spiritual information and manifests intellect and purpose. It is also where lower mind personality characteristics generated during incarnation are uploaded to and where those characteristics accumulate.

Higher mind's purpose: This is to integrate all gathered information, distil out repetition and redundancy, and come to clear mastery of everything associated with, related to, and implied by the accumulated information.

Higher self: The spiritual identity. It communicates with the lower self (that being the physical body and its brain) via the auric channel.

Human (conventional meaning): An individual consisting of body, social identity, mind and purpose.

Human (spiritual meaning): A spiritual identity, a node fragment of Dao-consciousness, who is either in an embodied or disembodied state.

Humanity (steady-state model): This transmission proposes that an endless and continuous stream of spiritual identity is cast from the Dao, some of which elect to mature and become refined by engaging in a process of repeated incarnation within the crucible offered by human existence on this planet. This process is beyond the comprehension of the human mind, and so cannot be defined by, or limited to, the human concepts of past or future. This renders meaningless all issues concerning end-times and related eschatological phenomena.

Identity (spiritual): Modelled as an essentially invisible sphere with a small kernel at its centre. It exists as a structure in agapéic space where it is able to move at will, but to a degree dependent on its spiritual development.

Imaginal: A term adopted by French Sufi scholar, Henry Corbin, in his attempt to explain the nature of mystical perceptions. Imaginal perceptions are both real and constructed, real in the sense that actual perceptions occur, and constructed insofar as when the lower mind attempts to make sense of those perceptions it interprets them using previously inculcated concepts and assumptions.

Implicate order: A subtle underlying component of reality proposed by physicist David Bohm. Here identified as part of the electrospiritual. It manifests in the auric level structure necessarily associated with any living organism.

Individual (social): A single human being separate and distinct from others.

Individual (spiritual): A node of Dao-consciousness.

Intellect: That aspect of mind which processes information.

Intention: That process of mind which elects, evaluates and subsequently intends a specific outcome.

Karma: The outcome of human reactions which result in others being radically disempowered, confined or killed.

Light (physical): Electromagnetic radiation to which the human eye is sensitive, nominally of wavelength 380-720nm.

Light (spiritual): A subtle perception of brightness derived via the auric perceptual channel. Generally correlated with agapéic frequency, that is, dim at lower frequency and brighter at higher frequency levels.

Love: A human biological level emotion, in contrast to agapé, which is experienced at the spiritual level.

Lower mind: A function of the biological brain, it processes information and manifests habitual emotional characteristics that result from imprinting and enculturation.

Memory (state dependent): In altered states of awareness experiences and perceptions generate memories that are not automatically accessed during ordinary states of awareness, i.e. attention focused at a lower mind level isn't able to access memories held at the higher mind level.

Mind: See *Higher mind* and *Lower mind*.

GLOSSARY

Model: A hypothetical description of a complex entity or process. A representation of something, sometimes on a smaller scale.

Multiverse: An extended experiment consisting of a small, undetermined number of universes, projected out of the ultimate unmanifest, each with its defining parameters, that expand and contract through an unspecified number of cycles before returning to the ultimate unmanifest.

Node: A zone of concentration of some attribute.

Node of Dao-consciousness: A condition of concentrated consciousness within the unmanifest absolute that contains intellect and purpose.

observer: The intent of the Dao that may be thought of as a large-scale emergent node of Dao-consciousness containing intellect and purpose. The unobserved initiator of the multiverse.

Point of attention: A product of focussed awareness, free to move without limit of space or time.

Purpose: See *Higher mind's purpose*.

Realm: This transmission proposes, in its model of agapéic space, that there are 100,000 discrete levels of agapéic frequency. Each level is a realm that provides a possible location for a node of Dao-consciousness comprising spiritual identity, and typically, for a population of such nodes.

Reify: Making something abstract more concrete or real. Religions originate in ephemeral spiritual experiences. To elucidate those experiences followers create rituals to echo them and doctrines to explain them. Over time, as exegesis is added to doctrines, worshippers' attention is displaced further and further from their religion's original ephemeral experiences. This is how religions reify their founders' spiritual experiences.

Reincarnation: Fundamental to the spiritual perspective offered here. It is proposed that each human identity incarnates an average of 1,000 times, using the opportunities to experience, learn, develop skills and understanding, all culminating in achieving a state of knowing, loving wisdom.

Religion: An informal or formalised organisation providing social engagement in a common interest. That interest is normally directed towards non-physical existence in order to contextualise human life.

Self: See *Higher self; Identity* and *Individual*.

Sensitivity: The ability to respond to stimuli or to register small differences in stimuli.

Sentience: The readiness to perceive sensations. Also indicates an elementary or undifferentiated consciousness.

Soul (group): In undivided form, the node of Dao-consciousness. In divided form, a cluster of fragments, more commonly known as individual souls or spirits, each of which incarnates individually in order to gather information. At the end of the cycle of incarnations the fragments re-unite to form a mature and refined node of Dao-consciousness. This transmission comes from such a re-united group soul.

Soul (individual): A traditional religious term. Here it is redefined as the fragment of a node of Dao-consciousness. This node fragment manifests as and is comprised of a spirit-sphere that co-associates with a human animal body, coalescing with it and thereby animating it.

Spirit: See *Soul* and *Spirit-sphere*.

Spirit sphere: An individual fragment of a node of Dao-consciousness in globular form. In human beings it manifests at the hara-level structure and defines individual human identity. It may only be observed via non-physical visual perception using the auric channel.

Spiritual identity: A node or node fragment of Dao-consciousness.

Spiritual realm: The Dao, including all manifest and unmanifest existence.

Spirituality: The idea or act of attending to a generally invisible domain of reality. Defined in different ways historically by religions and cultures.

Survival: When a physical body dies its associated lower mind dies with it. What survives is the information gathered during incarnation, and the spiritual self and its higher mind to which that information is uploaded.

Teaching (spiritual): A knowledge-set deliberately transferred from identity in spirit to lower mind in body.

The Real: A historical concept that proposes the spiritual domain is more significant and real than the physical domain. That is not supported here.

Time (disrupted or missing): Accessing the higher mind's level of awareness is normally associated with apparent disruptions or discontinuities in the ordinary awareness of passing time. This is a consequence of the functioning of bio-consciousness, not of Dao-consciousness.

Transmission (spiritual): A spiritually initiated transfer from a higher mind to a lower mind, usually comprising knowledge of spiritual existence, of physical existence from a spiritual perspective, and the relations between them.

Further Reading

Attar Books appreciates our readers' support. We request you consider posting an online review where you bought this book.

The following books offer further detail on the topics discussed here. We recommend the first two books particularly, the first being introductory, the second offering more technical detail.

LEARNING WHO YOU ARE

Learning Who You Are offers a contemporary take on the age-old questions of who we are and why we are here. The book builds on current scientific knowledge to show how the physical and spiritual realms are interlinked.

It does this by presenting a number of innovative models and conceptual frameworks that mesh with twenty-first century understanding. The book also discusses the process of validating these models and concepts empirically, through observation, and explains how meditation may be used to expand vision within and beyond the everyday self. Throughout, the emphasis is on practical processes, focused on the here and now, yet which have the potential to open a doorway into the beyond.

All this is explored using an

open-ended, experimental approach that challenges the rigid dichotomies of the past, such as the mundane many vs the enlightened few, and the profane human vs the sacred divine. Historically, the notion of divinity has erected a barrier between humanity and the spiritual realm, which signals that whatever happens in the spiritual dimension is distant and so must remain an unfathomable mystery. *Learning Who You Are* alternatively, and controversially, asserts that the spiritual domain is not divine; individual human spirits, enlightened or otherwise, are not special; and the spiritual is neither distant nor unfathomable.

The absence of divinity means no Divine Being is pushing or pulling any of us during the course of our lives. So understanding the fundamental nature of our existence doesn't depend on divine decree or sacred revelation. We are already spiritual, hence appreciating the spiritual bases of our existence may be achieved straightforwardly—should we wish to do so, and be willing to make the effort required to discern them.

Learning Who You Are offers the spiritually inquisitive and adventurous a unique, contemporary perspective on what it is to be human, and what may be achieved while living on this often perplexing planet.

THE KOSMIC WEB

The Kosmic Web offers fuller explanations of many concepts presented in introductory form in this book. It begins at the beginning, with the creation of the multiverse, then discusses the seeding of ecosystems, biological life and humanity. It goes on to explore many of the concepts introduced in these pages, but in much greater detail, specifically: the nature of Dao, the nature of the electrospiritual, the function of the aura, and the evolution of nodes and node fragments. It concludes with a consideration of the traditional Great Chain of Being, which is updated into the concept of the web of life. *The Kosmic Web* is recommended as the primary text for appreciating the guides' view of existence.

"The nature of the body, including its basic shape and functioning, is well known. What is not well known is the nature and shape of the spiritual identity that locates itself beside, within and through the body. The individual spiritual identity, and we are talking now in an energetic sense, exists in the shape of a sphere. Its structure is globular. Imagine a ball, say a soccer ball, with the hexagons and pentagons forming a net around its surface. Now imagine every intersection on that ball connected radially both inwards and outwards, forming a three-dimensional structure consisting of cellular interconnecting filaments. Here the image of the hexagonal walls of honeycomb inside a beehive are appropriate. The cellular structure inside the spirit sphere is patterned like the beehive, but much less rigidly, certainly not hexagonally, and the filaments extend inwards and outwards throughout the entire globular structure. The interconnecting filaments provide the means by which encoded information is carried through the entire structure.

Encoded within the spiritual identity's globular structure is information regarding what has been done in previous lives and what is intended to be achieved in the new upcoming life. How is information regarding the life plan communicated by the spiritual self to its animal human self? The answer is via the aura. So when a spiritual identity dispatches an aspect of itself into the human realm, the now born and growing human being can access knowledge of all the information encoded in its globular spiritual structure via the aura.

When the body dies and is incinerated or decays, the aura itself dissolves. But in the process of dissolving, all the information contained within the mind of the individual's human physical self is spontaneously uploaded, to use that modern concept, as patterns of information conveyed to the globular spiritual identity through the connecting link of the aura. This is easily achieved, because the identity is bi-located, with its spiritual self and its bodily self nested beside and inside one another. There is no distance for the information to travel. The uploading is direct, spontaneous and instantaneous."

THE MATAPAUA CONVERSATIONS

This book is the first collaboration between Peter and Keith. The circumstances that led to its creation is that after editing Peter's *Guided Healing*, Keith saw an opportunity to exploit Peter's contact with non-embodied identities to question them about the big bang, evolution, the nature of consciousness, and other metaphysical topics. He eventually came up with a list of one hundred "big questions".

Peter took time out at Matapaua Beach to receive the answers. He also kept a diary on the process. The excerpt that follows was spoken to Peter by the guides soon after he arrived at the secluded house where he stayed while channelling the answers to Keith's questions.

"We begin the developmental and systematic aspects of this teaching, fostered and communicated by the man Keith Hill. Given that it is at his request that we respond to his questions, we feel that proper acknowledgement should be made to the facilitative agreement that he has with us and with you. This agreement was made pre-life, of course.

When contemplating engagement with the earthly realm, you both felt there was an opportunity to contribute to a deeper understanding of the human condition. The opportunity was undertaken in a spirit of self-exploration and self-development. It also involved community engagement and company-inspired social development—"company" in this sense is to be interpreted as meaning a social group whose members share a curiosity concerning the dynamics of life and existence.

That said, we may continue in our task. Rereading Capra [Editor: Peter was reading *The Tao of Physics* by Fritjof Capra] is an essential first step for entering an analytical mindset and re-igniting your curiosity regarding the deep domains of description concerning both agapéic space and the realm of reality associated with the questions that you have come here to have answered.

The domain of these questions is extensive. Answering them requires that a boundary-free condition be established within your mind. That is not yet available, so we have set you the task of attending to the explanatory language offered in that text [*The Tao of Physics*] to take your awareness away from the mundane, away from the local, away from the body's senses and preferences, and expanding your awareness towards the foreign, and even the nonsensical. We use that last term in the special sense of being unrelated to the senses.

The mind is, in fact, free to soar into any realm at any moment, for any duration, within any time frame. This means that all of existence is accessible to the unconstrained mind. The frameworks of thought generated by locality, by embodiment, by emotion, by relationship—all these act to constrain the mind and its reach.

That is why self-isolation is required, to bring those unconstrained realms into view. That also gives rise to the need here to have mind-expanding literature at hand to refocus, as you did earlier when observing the night sky, because your perception is then not confined to the atmosphere. And it serves to remind that there are realms upon realms of distance, of phenomena, of locations far away, of unimaginable magnitudes, waiting the tools to make them observable. Those tools (for example, a telescope) are not available here. But the exercise was sufficient to remind him of the extent to which the world is bigger than this room, this body, these emotions, and these thoughts. The universe is correspondingly larger. The realm of all that is is unimaginably larger again. So, through this reminder, we bring that entire realm back into the central awareness as the vista to be explored during our time here."

ON ACQUIRING WISDOM

Traditionally, acquiring wisdom has involved becoming wise in the ways of the world and developing deep insight into what drives human existence. Notable among the wise in the Western tradition are Solomon, in whose

name Jewish wisdom literature was composed, and Pythagoras, whose enquiries led him to invent the word philosophy, a composite of two Greek words, philo (love) and sophia (wisdom). Pythagorean philosophy has two major themes: that number, not divine power, structures the world, and that we reincarnate repeatedly with the goal of acquiring wisdom.

On Acquiring Wisdom: A reincarnational perspective is a philosophic work in the Pythagorean sense, written to accord with our contemporary outlook. The discussions include using current terminology to redefine how we acquire wisdom, examining our purpose in reincarnating, weighing how our search for ecstasy, intimacy, serenity and balance are impeded and fostered, and the role of moral judgement in evaluating life choices. Models, some utilising number, show how progress may be identified and measured. Comment is also offered on post-death choices and the reluctance of some to disconnect themselves from their most recent life.

This is a book for those who are looking for a deep dive into what propels their existence. It is a thought-provoking work that combines metaphysical insights with pragmatic observations. The insights are sourced from a collective of human beings who have completed their incarnational cycles and are sharing their thoughts on humanity's spiritual dimension.

AGAPÉ AND THE HIERARCHY OF LOVE

Peter's first channelled book uses a wide range of models and metaphors to explore agapé theory. The overall thrust is scientific and secular, reconceiving traditional spiritual concepts in fresh and frequently innovative ways that are consistent with our modern outlook. Topics include the nature of the higher self and its mind and how to establish a connection to it, the thousand life incarnation model, the spiritual nature of love, and an exploration of the implications of agapé theory using models of many different kinds. The following is excerpted from the book's introduction.

"We intend to initiate an international movement towards the study of the impact of the spiritual domain on human life in all its variety, in particular its impact on the theory of being. Where once ground-level knowledge relevant to agriculture for food creation was sufficient, now theory has encompassed the origins and end of the known universe.

The question, then, is what lies beyond that? It was once enough to respond to the heart-felt love emanating from the spiritual domain, which people experienced via visions and in dreams. Now a more dynamic understanding is available that provides direct knowledge of the entities who inhabit the spiritual domain.

Once the current arguments regarding the existence of the spiritual domain are resolved, and a new consensual reality is established that draws on the empirical observations of mystics, a new inclusive outlook will arise. This will make a complete view of reality, that integrates the spiritual and the physical, available to anyone willing to take the time to develop the skills needed to perceive it. Religion in unsophisticated forms will fall away, as simplistic belief will not be required."

GUIDED HEALING

Guided Healing contains two urgent messages. One presents guidance for all spiritual seekers, the other is addressed specifically to potential healers.

To spiritual seekers, *Guided Healing* presents a novel view of the spiritual purpose and benefits of being born into a physical body. Issues covered include the relationship between the spiritual and physical realms, the reason for incarnation, the use of meditation as a means for exploring the spiritual realm, and the significance of soul work.

To healers, *Guided Healing* offers instruction on how to become a conduit for healing energy that emanates from the spiritual realm. Topics covered include how to contact guides in the spiritual realm, the nature of spiritual perception, and factors which enhance or hinder energy flow during the act of healing.

Most significantly, the text introduces the concept of agapéic space as a way to discuss spiritual existence and humanity's role in it. It reveals how agapé – spiritual love – underlies all existence, and what is required of us in order to tune into it.

Using concepts drawn from science and contemporary culture, Guided Healing presents a vision of human spirituality appropriate for our times, as we move out of traditional, paternalistic religious allegories and into a rational appreciation of what being spiritual involves.

PEOPLE OF THE EARTH

People of the Earth offers a unique account of communications with spiritual identities normally invisible to us: deceased people lost between worlds, nature spirits who nurture the Earth's ecosystems, and non-human beings who "drop in" to see what is going on. It challenges our assumptions regarding life and death, and asks us to reconsider who else may be sharing the universe with us.

When Peter Calvert gathered a small group of meditators and set them the task of opening their minds to whoever arrived, he didn't anticipate the astonishing encounters that would result. They discovered a small percentage of

people become confused after death. Lost in a transitional zone, they need guidance to move on to the next phase of their existence.

And in a series of vexed visits, nature spirits pleaded with the meditators to share an urgent message with humanity regarding the dire state of the planet's ecosystems.

Through a sequence of intriguing dialogues between the meditators and visiting non-embodied beings, *People of the Earth* provides insights to those who seek to understand what is required of us spiritually to sustain the planet's health.

"I have always considered the nature of our embodiment the most important unresolved issue of our civilisation. Peter Calvert and his colleagues have made an ambitious attempt to communicate with disembodied life forms. The fact that these dialogues are of varying clarity, alien credibility, and internal continuity is not as important as the acts of faith that generated them. The urgent truth is that we have to begin somewhere if we are going to explore tabooed portals, claim our place in the greater universe, and find the wisdom necessary to redeem our own world."
— Richard Grossinger, author of *The Night Sky: Soul and Cosmos* and *Bottoming Out the Universe: Why Is There Something Rather Than Nothing?*

www.ingramcontent.com/pod-product-compliance
Lightning Source LLC
Chambersburg PA
CBHW030336010526
44119CB00047B/513